The Big Book
of More
Sports Insults

The Big Book of More Sports Insults

Jonathan L'Estrange

WEIDENFELD & NICOLSON

Weidenfeld & Nicolson
Wellington House, 125 Strand, London WC2R 0BB

First published 2005

A CIP record for this book is available from the British
Library

ISBN 0304 36810 5

Design by www.carrstudio.co.uk

Printed in Great Britain by Clays Ltd, St Ives plc

www.orionbooks.co.uk

Contents

Foreword   7

Football Carry on Effing!   11

Cricket It's not natural, is it?   149

Rugby Union Cauliflower ears and arse-slapping   237

Tennis Wham, bam, thank you ma'am   271

Golf Boulevard of broken dreams   303

US Sports Who are they trying to kid?   315

Other sports (Mostly minor ones)   325

Picture credits   350

FOREWORD

The Big Book of More Sports Insults is a sequel to *The Big Book of Sports Insults*, published in October 2004. The earlier book having gobbled up the lion's share of 'classic' sporting insults from a whole century of sporting activity, much of the present volume inevitably has a somewhat narrower chronological focus, and contains a higher proportion of material relating to recent sporting events than did its predecessor.

A year is a long time in sport: at the end of 2004 Australia's cricketers were universally hailed as the world's best (the imminent arrival on British shores of the terrifying Adam Gilchrist and his marauding mates was anticipated with the kind of dread our ancestors must have felt prior to a visit from a longboat crammed with sex-starved Viking warriors); in football an aura of invincibility still clung to Arsenal football club and its then apparently cool and unflappable manager – while the idea of Liverpool winning a fifth European Cup was associated more with members of the Merseyside chapter of the Flat Earth Society than with reasoned commentators. But 2005 was to be a year in which – Tiger Woods and Roger Federer excepted – the glorious uncertainty of sport triumphantly re-asserted itself. *The Big Book of More Sports Insults* devotes generous coverage to the sometimes astounding events of this sporting twelvemonth – from Wales's plausibility-defying rugby union grand slam, via Liverpool's form-book-overturning night on the Bosphorus, to the coronary-inducing events of the 2005 Ashes series.

As befits a globally dominant sport, football occupies the largest number of pages in the selection that follows. The ubiquity of the sport in the broadcast and print media ensures a steady flow of quotable material, and the high passions the game engenders guarantee a generally exalted level of bile. It must be said, however, that when it comes to sheer quality of vituperation, the world's most popular sport (for all the cruel wit of its best terrace chants) is probably not quite top dog (or should that be top bitch?). No. The prize for 'Most Insult-provoking Sport' goes jointly to two apparently civilized English summer games – cricket and tennis. The former – thanks largely to the foul-mouthed efforts of its Antipodean practitioners – has given the world the not-so-subtle art of 'sledging' (see pages 225–230), while tennis… well, it just seems to bring out the bitch in everyone. Turn to pages 273–287 if you need convincing.

The Big Book of More Sports Insults repeats no material that appeared in the earlier *Big Book of Sports Insults*. Any reader who is unable to locate a favourite insult in the present volume is therefore advised, before berating its compiler, to try *The Big Book of Sports Insults*, where they may conceivably find it.

Jonathan L'Estrange
September 2005

FOOTBALL
Carry on Effing!

From a royal decree of 1314, banning football in London:

For as much as there is great noise in the city caused by hustling over large balls, from which many evils may arise, which God forbid, we command and forbid on behalf of the King, on pain of imprisonment, such games to be used.

King Edward II. His son Edward III would later order footballers to take up archery instead.

From this court I debarre all rough and violent exercises, as the foot-ball, meeter for laming than making able the users thereof.

King James I of Scotland issues an early yellow card to Duncan Ferguson, 1424.

Football's like a big market place, and people go to the market every day to buy their vegetables.

Sir Bobby Robson enters a metaphorical minefield; quoted on dangerhere.com.

On English football in the 2000s:

… a … grisly caricature of Thatcherite individualism.

Peter Oborne in the *Evening Standard*, 17 November 2003.

Football is … an increasingly powerful institution, pored over by millions, its stars fêted and worshipped like never before. Yet it is played, managed and run by violent thugs and cheats.
Chris Blackhurst in the *Evening Standard*, 4 February 2005.

As speculation grew over an alleged meeting between Arsenal's Ashley Cole and parties representing Chelsea:
To most of us, 'Football Club Makes Illegal Approach for Player' causes a similar level of astonishment to such other headlines as: 'Official: Prince Harry A Bit Of A Thickie'; or 'Revealed: Cherie Blair Not Averse To Making a Few Bob.'
Matthew Norman in the *Evening Standard*, 7 February 2005.

Twenty-two silly haircuts and three rape allegations.
William Donaldson and Hermione Eyre define 'the beautiful game', in *The Dictionary of National Celebrity* (2005).

I wouldn't hang a dog on the word of a footballer.
Alan Hardaker, former secretary of the Football League; quoted by Brian Glanville in *The Times*, 15 February 2005.

The fans — middle-class tossers?

Away from home our fans are fantastic, I'd call them the hardcore fans. But at home they have a few drinks and probably the prawn sandwiches, and they don't realize what's going on out on the pitch.

Roy Keane on corporate hospitality at Old Trafford, 1997. Keane's 2005 Manchester United salary of around £70,000 per week would buy him about 45,000 packs of Marks and Spencer's prawn and mayonnaise sandwiches.

Middle-class tossers who are ruining football.

A tongue-in-cheek dismissal of contemporary fans; in the *Guardian Guide to The Season 04/05*.

Two types of people go to football matches. The first group wear thick coats apparently made from boiler lagging and arrive at least half-an-hour before kick-off … The second group wear only the flimsiest shirt no matter what the weather and keep warm by a combination of beer and layers of aftershave. This group never gets to the ground until 30 seconds before kick-off.

Harry Pearson in the *Guardian Guide to The Season 04/05*.

● FOOTBALLERS
Scum, total scum...

It's … the drunken parties
that go on for days – the orgies,
the birds and the fabulous money.

Former Arsenal midfielder Peter Storey, nicknamed 'Snout', sings the
praises of football in the 1970s.

Footballers are scum, total scum. They're bigger scum than journalists. They don't know what honesty or loyalty is. They're the biggest scum who walk on this planet and if they weren't football players, most of them would be in prison, it's as simple as that.

Alan Sugar, former chairman of Tottenham Hotspur, quoted by Brian Glanville in *The Times*, 15 February 2005.

Victims of a violent strain of Tourette's Syndrome.

Sue Mott on swearing footballers; in the *Daily Telegraph*, 9 March 2005.

Shock as footballer not arrested!

Spoof headline in *Private Eye*.

X downed a cocktail of beer, vodka and cigarette ash and then began eating parts of his mobile phone and was asked to leave. Outside he threw a bollard at a car. Meanwhile Y had removed his shirt, dropped his pants and was waving his genitalia at passers-by.

Two unnamed premiership footballers enjoy themselves inside and outside a 'northwest nightclub'; in the *Observer*, 8 May 2005.

Tony Adams

He used to turn like an oil tanker and run with the ball like a Keystone Cop.
The Rough Guide to Cult Football (2003).

Jingle bells, jingle bells, jingle all the way,
Oh what fun it is to see Adams put away, Oh…!
Opposing fans enjoy themselves at Adams's expense after the Arsenal player's encounter with a suburban brick wall.

Jérémie Aladière

He is the kind who would limp home from
A Question of Sport.
Evening Standard, 15 April 2005, on Arsenal's injury-dogged Frenchman.

Darren Anderton

John Gordon Sinclair looks so gawky he could be a natural for the movie 'Darren Anderton's Life Story'.
The Rough Guide to Cult Football (2003) compares Anderton to the star of the 1981 film *Gregory's Girl*.

Nicolas Anelka

The incredible sulk.
A nickname that has also been applied to Thierry Henry and the late Conservative prime minister Sir Edward Heath.

The French Craig Bellamy.
'Au revoir, Anelka', in the *Evening Standard*, 1 February 2005.

Alan Ball

You'd make a good little jockey.
Blackpool FC turn down a future hero of 1966.

Alan Ball, Alan Ball
He's a squeaky ginger bastard
And he's only three foot tall.
To the tune of 'Wem-ber-lee! Wem-ber-lee!', Manchester City fans
taunt their former manager.

Milan Baros

Baros and Garcia whipped off their alice bands like
a couple of secretaries discarding their spectacles
after a day in the typing pool, shaking free their
glossy locks in a day-to-evening transformation
that would have made Trinny and Susannah proud.
Jess Cartner-Morley, 'Liverpool's good hair day', in the *Guardian*,
5 May 2005; after Liverpool's defeat of Chelsea in the second leg of
the Champions League semi-final, 3 May 2005.

Fabien Barthez

He's French, he's shit,
His head's a fucking tit.
Oldham fans greet the shaven-headed former Manchester United
goalkeeper.

Joey Barton

After Barton jabbed a lit cigar into the eye of reserve team player
James Tandy when the latter tried to set fire to Barton's shirt at
Manchester City's 2004 fancy-dress Christmas party:
The most inappropriate use of a cigar since
Monica Lewinsky.
Daniel Taylor in the *Guardian*, 12 February 2005.

David Batty

Describing Batty and Le Saux's fisticuffs in a match in Moscow:
Batty and Le Saux there, arguing over who has the
sillier name.
Rory Bremner in the guise of Des Lynam, Channel 4, 1995.

Jim Baxter

Slim Jim had everything required of a great Scottish
footballer. Outrageously skilled, totally irrespons-
ible, supremely arrogant and thick as mince.
The Absolute Game (fanzine), 1990.

Peter Beardsley

Christ, he looks like a thin Ann Widdecombe.
Nicky Clarke, hairstylist; quoted in Phil Shaw, *The Book of Football Quotations* (2003 edition).

James Beattie

Beattie and Butt-head.
The name bestowed by journalists on the incident in which Everton's James Beattie headbutted Chelsea's William Gallas in the back of the neck, 12 February 2005.

Can't score on the pitch, can't score off the pitch either.
Anon. Evertonian quoted in the *Evening Standard*, 26 May 2005. A Sunday newspaper had reported on Beattie's encounter with one Jayne Evans during a night out with team-mates on the Costa de Sol. Beattie and Evans allegedly returned to Beattie's hotel room, where the former Southampton striker 'collapsed fully clothed on the bed before instantly falling asleep'.

David Beckham

Roy Keane has said that he will stay at Man United through thick and thin – or Becks and Posh, as they are known.
Rory Bremner, on BBC TV *They Think It's All Over*, 1999.

The face of an angel and the bum of a Greek god.
The gay magazine *Attitude* names Beckham its ultimate fantasy footballer, 1999.

Chris Eagles, 18, has been described as 'the new David Beckham', which overlooks the fact that he actually has the ability to go past people.
The *Guardian Guide to The Season 04/05* on the young Manchester United player.

Happy birthday, Oldenballs.
Chris Charles on bbc.co.uk, 2 May 2005, Beckham's 30th birthday.

¡Cruz a silly boy, then!

On the the Beckhams' choice of the forename 'Cruz' for their third son:

I think it is quite a stupid name, frankly. They will have problems in Spain because it will be seen as a name for girls. It is an old-fashioned girl's name and also it is quite clearly Spanish and difficult to pronounce for an English-speaking person. It is quite a strange thing to do to a little boy.
Lola Oria, a Spanish language tutor at Oxford University; quoted on bbc.co.uk, February 2005.

¡Learn Spanish the Beckham way!

El partido con Atletico was mucho mejor para todos.

Beckham attempts to say, in Spanish: 'The game against Atletico was much better for all of us.' The *Sun* later claimed that Beckham may have been fed his lines by Victoria Beckham via a listening device hidden under his white woolly hat; on bbc.co.uk.

Commenting on the complaint by Arrigo Sacchi, Real Madrid's director of football, that Beckham had failed to learn Spanish properly in two years at Real Madrid:

Quite why this should be such a surprise to Signor Sacchi is beyond me. Becks spent the previous 25 years residing in England without even coming close to fluency in his mother tongue.

Piers Morgan in the *Evening Standard*, 31 May 2005.

For someone who is still learning English, his Spanish is pretty good.

Phone-in caller to Radio Five Live, 30 May 2005.

¡Hable Ingles con Beckham!

On his family background:
My parents have always been there for me, ever since I was about seven.

After the birth of his first child:
We're definitely going to get Brooklyn christened, but we don't know into which religion.

Alex Ferguson is the best manager I've ever had at this level. Well, he's the only manager I've actually had at this level. But he's the best manager I've ever had.

When asked if he thought that he was a 'volatile' player:
Well, I can play in the centre, on the right and occasionally on the left side.

On receiving the OBE:
It's a great honour ... and it's an honour to be with Her Majesty, obviously ... I'm very honoured to be given this honour.

On being asked to name his favourite Olympic memories at the final London 2012 press conference:
Coe running barefoot.
(A muddled Beckham was possibly thinking of Zola Budd.)

On getting himself booked in England's World Cup qualifier against Wales, October 2004:
It was deliberate. I am sure some people think that I have not got the brains to be that clever, but I do have the brains.

By the way, there is no truth in the rumour that David Beckham is joining Newcastle. He says he won't go there given what the toon army just did to Asia.

Rodney Marsh puns on Sky Sports, January 2005, just weeks after a *tsunami* (tidal wave) killed more than 200,000 people in Indonesia, Thailand, Sri Lanka and India. Marsh's gag provoked much criticism and led to his being axed by Sky. Jim White commented primly in the *Daily Telegraph*: 'Marsh's gag was crass, juvenile and unfunny, which is standard for him' (27 January 2005).

It has recently been discovered that 'David and Victoria Beckham' form the anagram: 'Bravo! Victim and dickhead.'

William Donaldson and Hermione Eyre, *The Dictionary of National Celebrity* (2005).

Craig Bellamy

Craig was gobby with plenty of people, but then smaller lads generally are.

Gordon Strachan in the *Guardian*, 28 January 2005 (*see also* Textual Intercourse, page 61).

A mouthy serial delinquent with ... limited abilities as a striker.

David Mellor in the *Evening Standard*, 8 July 2005.

It's not so much that Craig Bellamy has a lack of class, it is more that he has no class whatsoever.
Tony Cascarino in *The Times*, 2 March 2005, after reports that Bellamy had ridiculed an opponent for earning less money than him. 'Apparently Bellamy told [Darren] Sheridan [a 37-year-old Clyde player] that he would be doing his gardening soon. Frankly, if Bellamy does have a gardener, he is probably smarter than his employer.'

Dennis Bergkamp

One British Airways,
There's only one British Airways...
Sung by Chelsea fans to the tune of Los Tres Paraguayos' 1970s hit 'Guantanamera' to taunt the Dutchman, notorious for his fear of flying.

George Best

So that's what you look like – I've played against you three times and all I've ever seen is your arse!
Welsh international left-back Graham Williams grabs Best's face after Northern Ireland's 3–2 defeat of Wales, 15 April 1964 (Best's international début).

Would you like another Stella, Georgie Best?
Would you like another Stella, Georgie Best
Would you like another Stella,
'Cos your face is turning yella,
Would you like another Stella,
Georgie Best?

To the tune of 'She'll Be Coming Round the Mountain', Manchester City fans celebrate the alcohol problems of the former Old Trafford legend. Further verses embrace a range of ales and spirits.

Igor Biscan

Supercroatigorbiscanusedtobeatrocious.
Banner waved by Liverpool fans during the Champions League final in Istanbul, 25 May 2005, in homage to the once-derided Croatian midfielder.

Luther Blissett

When Blissett left … Watford for Milan, the common perception was that the Italians, in true John Motson style, had got their black players mixed up and had meant to sign John Barnes.
The Rough Guide to Cult Football (2003) on the Watford and England player of the 1980s.

Stan Bowles

If Stan could pass a betting shop the way he can pass a ball he'd have no worries whatsoever.
Ernie Tagg, Bowles's manager at Crewe Alexandra, on a player who once said of himself 'I stopped training, except for running to the bookmaker's for the two o'clock race.'

Lee Bowyer

Bergkamp got away with a blatant slap of Lee Bowyer's face, for which we can only congratulate the Dutchman. Someone's got to do it, haven't they?
BBC Sport Online columnist, January 2003.

I have never met Lee Bowyer, but everyone I have spoken to about him says he is a toerag.
Tony Cascarino in *The Times*, 4 April 2005.

Lee Bowyer is the nastiest piece of work in sport –
a violent, foul-mouthed, horrible little lout.
Piers Morgan, after the Bowyer–Dyer punch-up, in the *Evening
Standard*, 5 April 2005.

Wayne Bridge

Russia's oil wealth used to put men in space. Now,
via Roman Abramovich, it helps keep Wayne
Bridge in beer, hotel rooms and Porsches.
The *Guardian Guide to The Season 04/05*, on Chelsea's underused
left-sided defender.

Eric Cantona

1966 was a great year for English football. Eric was
born.
Nike advertising slogan, 1994.

1995 was a great year for English football. Eric was
banned.
T-shirt slogan worn by various non-Manchester United fans after
Cantona's ban for kung-fu kicking a Crystal Palace fan, 1995.

Loony toons

Slog on the Tyne.
Nickname given to the punch-up between Lee Bowyer and his Newcastle team-mate Kieron Dyer during Newcastle's 3–0 home defeat by Aston Villa, 2 April 2005. Both players were sent off and Bowyer, who instigated the fracas, was fined six weeks' wages (about £250,000).

Loathsome Lee … Anger infests his simple mind. He could get sent off playing Solitaire.
Henry Winter in the *Daily Telegraph*, 4 April 2005.

My first reaction was delight that Alan Shearer's big day had been ruined.
Matthew Norman alludes to the fact that the Bowyer–Dyer punch-up happened during a game supposed to be a celebration of Alan Shearer's decision to postpone his retirement for another year; in the *Evening Standard*, 4 April 2005.

On those Newcastle fans who rose in tribute to Dyer and Bowyer in their first game back:
… soft-headed forgiveniks …
Sue Mott in the *Daily Telegraph*, 12 April 2005.

Jamie Carragher

It looks to me like he has cramp in both groins.
Andy Townsend reveals the amazing anatomical secret behind
Carragher's transformation into a world-class defender; ITV
commentary on the Champions League final, 25 May 2005.

Roy Carroll

The last 'Roy' from the northwest to cause so
much hilarity wore a helmet and goggles and went
by the name of Chubby Brown.
Matt Hughes and Raoul Simons, Football Focus in the *Evening
Standard*, 25 February 2005. A Carroll bungle had gifted AC Milan a
1–0 victory over Manchester United at Old Trafford in the Champions
League.

Carroll not-so-Smiley.
The *Evening Standard* puns after the same incident.

Bobby Charlton

I sent my son to one of his schools of excellence
and he came back bald.
George Best on the *Mrs Merton Show*, 1996.

Djibril Cissé

[He has] … a street map of Surbiton carved onto his scalp.

Giles Smith in *The Times*, 5 May 2005.

Ashley Cole

Runs fast, smiles a lot, struggles in defence. Only plays for England because he's not Phil Neville.

Simon Burnton on the pre-Euro 2004 Ashley Cole, in the *Guardian Guide to The Season 04/05*.

Colegate.

The inevitable nickname attached to Chelsea representatives' alleged meeting with Ashley Cole, a contracted Arsenal player, in the Royal Park Hotel in West London, January 2005. Arsenal's chairman, Peter Hill-Wood, expressed outrage at the 'tapping up' of one of their players.

Joe Cole

He has always been a slippery little git.

Rio Ferdinand pays tribute to his former West Ham team-mate, quoted on bbc.co.uk, spring 2005.

Stan Collymore

The articulate dogger.

On sport.guardian.co.uk/smalltalk.

Peter Crouch

He's tall, he's lean,
He's a freaky goal machine,
Peter Crouch, Peter Crouch.

Sung by Norwich fans when Crouch played at Carrow Road while on
loan from Aston Villa.

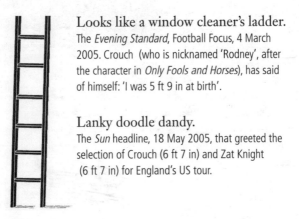

Looks like a window cleaner's ladder.

The *Evening Standard*, Football Focus, 4 March
2005. Crouch (who is nicknamed 'Rodney', after
the character in *Only Fools and Horses*), has said
of himself: 'I was 5 ft 9 in at birth'.

Lanky doodle dandy.

The *Sun* headline, 18 May 2005, that greeted the
selection of Crouch (6 ft 7 in) and Zat Knight
(6 ft 7 in) for England's US tour.

Ed de Goey

We want a 'tache like Ed de Goey,
Super Dutch porn star.

Stoke City fans welcome the former Chelsea goalkeeper, to the tune
of 'London Bridge is Falling Down.'

Paolo di Canio

Explaining the Italian's controversial raised-arm salute to Lazio fans after a derby win over Roma:

He says, 'I went down to say hello to my supporters.'

Paolo di Canio's agent Matteo Roggi, January 2005; quoted on bbc.co.uk. Far-right politician Alessandra Mussolini, granddaughter of the former Italian dictator, said of di Canio's gesture: 'How nice that Roman salute was, it delighted me so much. I shall write him a thank-you note.' Lazio's fascist associations arise from its having been Benito Mussolini's favourite club. Di Canio has the tattoo DUX on his arm (*dux* being Latin for *duce*, leader).

Poor lad. Like all Lazio supporters, he is just not used to winning.

Maurizio Gasparri, Italian telecommunications minister and Roma supporter, takes a charitable view of di Canio's action; quoted on bbc.co.uk, 9 January 2005.

Julian Dicks

See West Ham United (page 94).

Referees bug-eyed baldies and preening popinjays

On Pierluigi Collina:

The bug-eyed baldie.

Russell Kempson in *The Times*, 9 March 2005.

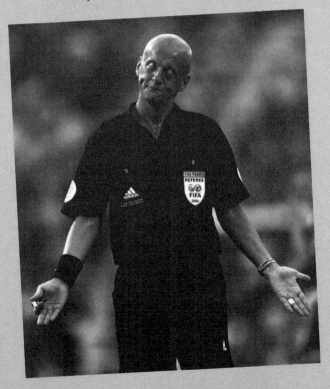

On Anders Frisk:

A preening popinjay with a long-established habit of cosying up to the big teams … a buffoon.
David Mellor on the perma-tanned Swede, in the *Evening Standard*, 25 February 2005, following Chelsea's second-round Champions League defeat by Barcelona at the Camp Nou, in which Frisk controversially sent off Chelsea's Didier Drogba.

I would like Frisk as the ref. Perhaps he would help us like the way he helped [Barcelona] in Spain.
José Mourinho, 7 March 2005, refuting an allegation by UEFA that he had called for Pierluigi Collina to be referee for the return leg of Chelsea's Champions League tie with Barcelona on 8 March. Chelsea earlier claimed that Barcelona coach Frank Rijkaard entered Frisk's dressing-room at half-time during the first leg, shortly before Frisk sent off Drogba.

On Graham Poll:

I didn't know you were a Spurs fan.
Blackburn Rovers manager Graeme Souness to Poll during a Blackburn v. Tottenham match; quoted on bbc.co.uk. Souness was promptly given his marching orders.

On Rob Styles:

Type the words "Rob", "Styles" and "controversy" into Google together and there are 10,500 results from the UK.
Stuart James in the *Evening Standard*, 17 May 2005.

El-Hadji Diouf

The dive performed by Diouf … has taken the art form to a new level.

Oliver Kay in *The Times*, 26 January 2005, following the Senegalese striker's blatant (and penalty-winning) dive against Blackburn Rovers at Ewood Park.

The Bolton striker was surprisingly omitted from the Best Actor category in this week's Oscar nominations, but, given his theatrical tumble against Blackburn on Monday, a BAFTA is the least he deserves.

Football Focus in the *Evening Standard*, 28 January 2005.

Some younger fans have taken to calling him 'Dufus', apparently American street slang for idiot.

David Mellor in the *Evening Standard*, 28 January 2005.

Doudou Ebeu Mbombo

There was that lad Doudou who played for QPR and most weeks that summed up his performance. His mate Shittu, on the other hand, isn't as bad as he sounds.

Derek 'Robbo' Robson, 'The Tees Mouth', on bbc.co.uk.

C'mon, do the Dudek with me!

He looked like a starfish with jelly legs – he modernized my spaghetti legs.

Bruce Grobbelaar, whose wobbly-kneed routine helped distract Roma in Liverpool's penalty shoot-out win in the 1984 European Cup final, salutes Jerzy Dudek after Liverpool's penalty shoot-out victory in the 2005 Champions League final. At Jamie Carragher's prompting, Dudek did his own version of Grobbelaar's rubber-legged routine. Three AC Milan penalty takers duly fluffed their shots, thereby transforming error-prone Pole into Anfield legend; quoted in *The Times*, 27 May 2005.

The Dudek Dance is a craze sweeping the nightclubs of Italy. It's based on the idiosyncratic jig Dudek performed in goal every time AC Milan were about to take a penalty in the Champions League final last month.

The *Guardian*, June 2005.

Jerzy Dudek

… a byword for comedy keepers.
The Times, 27 May 2005.

Kieron Dyer

After Dyer had been caught on a CCTV camera 'urinating in an alleyway':

If you ever do anything like this again, I will bin you.
Graeme Souness to Kieron Dyer as he accompanied the latter to a police station to receive a caution, October 2004; quoted in the *Observer*, 3 April 2005.

Football's 'king of bling'.
Henry Winter in the *Daily Telegraph*, 4 April 2005.

From the government's records of the two companies recorded in Dyer's name at Companies House:

For Mario Promotions:
– 'Director: Kieron Dyer,
Occupation: Professional Footballer'.
For Fieldmount Properties Limited:
– 'Director: Kieron Dyer,
Occupation: Serial Roaster'.
Quoted in the *Observer*, 10 April 2005.

Rio Ferdinand

What can one say about a man who once damaged a tendon while watching TV with his feet on a coffee table?
Anon. football journalist, 2003.

Ri-o, you should have pissed in the cup.

A warm Wolverhampton welcome for the Manchester United defender, sung to the tune of 'Blue Moon'.

Chelsea rent-boy.

Chanted by some Manchester United fans during Manchester United's 4–0 defeat of Charlton Athletic, 1 May 2005. Following a well-publicized meeting with Chelsea's chief executive Peter Kenyon, Ferdinand had still to agree the terms of a new contract with Manchester United.

Wannabe-gangsta, faux-rapper, Peckham wideboy Lothario schtick.

Red Issue, a Manchester United fanzine, sums up what it does not like about Rio Ferdinand, April 2005.

One minute he can't produce any urine. The next he's extracting it.

Matt Lawton in the *Daily Mail*, 17 May 2005, alluding to Ferdinand's infamous missed drugs test in 2003 and to his 2005 pay demands.

Diego Forlan

Diego Forlorn.

Nickname accorded the Uruguayan by his critics during his spell at Manchester United (for whom Forlan took 28 games to score his first goal). In addition to his 17 goals in 98 games (61 as a substitute), Forlan spawned one new Old Trafford chant after a double strike to defeat Liverpool: 'He came from Uruguay and made the Scousers cry.'

William Foulke

It's often said that goalkeepers fill the goal. At 24 stone, Foulke genuinely did.

The Rough Guide to Cult Football (2003) on the turn of the 19th-century Chelsea and England goalkeeper 'Fatty' Foulke ('a leviathan … with the agility of a bantam').

Luis Garcia

He looks like a surly hairdresser.

Matt Hughes on Liverpool's Spanish striker, in the *Evening Standard*, 4 May 2005 (*see also* Milan Baros, page 18).

Paul Gascoigne

A man capable of breaking both leg and wind at
the same time.
Jimmy Greaves in the *Sun* newspaper, 1996.

If ye cannae beat the Ajax beat yir wife.
Sung by Celtic fans when Gazza was a Rangers player, c.1996.

Steven Gerrard

I apologize for introducing an ugly word like
prickteaser into a high-minded column, but how
else can I properly describe the antics of Steven
Gerrard?
David Mellor on the will-he-won't-he saga that preceded Gerrard's
decision to remain at Anfield rather than move to Chelsea; 'Oh Stevie,
you crafty little tease', in the *Evening Standard*, 8 July 2005.

… I spat my cornflakes out all over the table.
Jamie Carragher on his reaction to Gerrard's decision to stay at
Liverpool; quoted in 'Overheard…', in the *Guardian*, 9 July 2005.

Jimmy Greaves

Responding to the question 'who was the biggest influence on your
career?':
Vladimir Smirnoff.
Jimmy Greaves, interview with *Loaded* magazine, 1995. His TV
colleague Ian St John had replied 'Bill Shankly' to the same question.

Perry Groves

He had hair so orange it could surely be seen from space.

The Rough Guide to Cult Football (2003) on the former Arsenal winger.

Eidur Gudjohnsen

An erratic nitwit.

David Mellor in the *Evening Standard*, 11 February 2005.

Thierry Henry — France's finest whines

The most facially expressive Frenchman since Marcel Marceau.

Matt Hughes in the *Evening Standard*, 2 March 2005.

The whine merchant.

Matt Hughes.

The ability to communicate the phrase 'This is somebody else's fault' with no more than a flicker of an eybrow makes him a world-beater of sorts.

Simon Burnton in the *Guardian Guide to The Season 04/05*.

There's no finer sight than when he opens his legs and just comes on the ball.

Terry Paine, commentating on South African television, July 2005.

Ruud Gullit

My pot-bellied pigs don't squeal as much as him.
Vinnie Jones after being sent off for a foul on Ruud Gullit, 1995;
quoted in the *Book of Football Quotations* (2003 edition).

Alf-Inge Haaland

I fucking hit him hard.
Roy Keane brags about his tackle on Haaland (April 2001) in his
autobiography (2002). Keane was fined £150,000 and banned for
five games (*see also* page 46).

John Hamilton

The time has come, Mr Hamilton, for you to
rejoin your teeth.
Referee Tom Wharton sends off the argumentative Heart of Midlothian
left-winger of the 1960s during a match against Hibernian. The
combative 'Hammie' had, through various accidents, lost his own
teeth, and kept his dentures in his locker during matches; quoted in
Wharton's obituary in the *Independent*, 16 May 2005.

Paul Heckingbottom

Crazy name, crazy guy ... In the few games he
played, he looked like someone who'd strolled in
from the chip shop.
The *Guardian Guide to The Season 04/05* on the former Norwich City
player.

Tim Howard

Timmy Howard
Fuck off!
He's got Tourette's.

A Manchester United chant alluding to the profanity-inducing
neurological disorder that afflicts their American goalkeeper.

Petr the Great against Yank the Plank.

Matt Hughes compares Chelsea's safe-as-houses goalkeeper Petr Cech
with Manchester United's inconsistent American, whose blunder
helped Chelsea to victory in the Carling Cup semi-final; in the *Evening
Standard*, 27 January 2005. 'Tim's a bit Dim', ran the *Sun*'s headline.

Lee Hughes

Drink when you're driving,
You only drink when you're driving.

To the tune of 'Guantanamera', West Ham fans taunt West Brom fans
after striker Lee Hughes was arrested on a charge of causing death by
dangerous driving (Hughes was jailed for six years in August 2004).

David James

David names *The Hobbit* as his all-time fave [book] … Apparently he has been reading Tolkien for 17 years and has just reached page 36 because – and yes, yes, I know you've seen it coming – every time he goes to pick it up, it slips through his fingers.

Matthew Norman in the *Evening Standard*, 4 April 2005. Players from each premiership club had agreed to help a new campaign for literacy by naming their favourite books.

Leighton James

Your pace is very deceptive. You're even slower than you look.

Derby County manager Tommy Docherty to the Welsh winger, 1977.

Nkwankwo Kanu

He's tall, he's black,
He's had a heart attack,
Kanu, Kanu…

Arsenal fans salute the Nigerian, who has experienced cardiac problems in the past, c.2000 (*see also* The Animal XI, page 63).

Roy Keane

On Keane's infamous 'tackle' on Manchester City's Alf-Inge Haaland:

An inhuman lunge that was more assault than tackle.

John Aizlewood in the *Sunday Times*, 6 February 2005 (*see also* page 43).

See also Patrick Vieira (page 66), According to Clough (page 100), and Mick McCarthy (page 109).

Martin Keown

Martin Keown is up everybody's backside.

Trevor Brooking salutes the tenacious Keown, *Match of the Day* commentary, 1996.

Harry Kewell

Can you believe that people were actually queueing up to buy him not so long ago?

Derek 'Robbo' Robson, The Tees Mouth, on bbc.co.uk, May 2005.

Good to see that Kewell has spent his time out of the squad growing his hair into the perfect chin-length bob, the better to carry off the alice band.

Jess Cartner-Morley, 'Liverpool's good hair day', in the *Guardian*, 5 May 2005.

If all Aussies were this fragile, England would be odds-on to regain the Ashes this summer.

Wayne Veysey in the *Evening Standard*, 26 May 2005. Kewell limped out of Liverpool's Champions League final against AC Milan after just 20 minutes, complaining about an injury that no-one could remember him sustaining.

A player with a heart the size of a diamond ear-stud.

Richard Williams on a player he also referred to as 'the Australian dilettante'; in the *Guardian*, 27 May 2005.

Graeme Le Saux

Le Saux is vilified for a secret much more shameful than being a homosexual. Le Saux is middle-class.

Ian Hislop, 1999. *See also* David Batty (page 19).

Glen Little

He dropped out at 1 p.m. when we discovered he had tweaked a hamstring walking upstairs at home. We're now asking him to move to a bungalow.

Steve Coppell, the Reading manager, on Little's late withdrawal from the match against Brighton and Hove Albion. Reading still won 2–1; quoted in *The Times*, quotes of the year, 2004.

Mind the moose! a trio of bizarre injuries

Darren Bernard of Barnsley: slipped in a puddle of urine left by a puppy and was sidelined for several months with knee ligament damage.

Svein Grondralen of Norway: had to withdraw from an international match after colliding with a moose while out jogging.

Alex Stepney of Manchester United: dislocated his jaw shouting at his defence.

In *The Rough Guide to Cult Football* (2003).

Ally McCoist

There's only one John Parrott!
Celtic fans serenade the Rangers hero and *Question of Sport* panellist in his last professional game.

Steve McManaman

You won't see that again now the Scouser's got it!
Ron Atkinson as the former Liverpool player raises the 2002 European Champions Cup for Real Madrid, ITV commentary.

Diego Maradona

Gwaaaagghhhhhooooooooool!
Gwaaaagghhhhhooooooooool!
Gwaaaagghhhhhooooooooool!
Diegooooooooooooooooo! Maradoooooooooona!
The greatest player of all time! ... From what
planet did you come? ... Argentina two, England
nil! Diegooooooooool! Diegooooooooool! Diego
Armando Maradona! ... Thank you, God, for
football ... for Maradona ... for these tears, for ...
this ... Argentina two, England ... nil.

Ectasy for Argentinians; the ultimate insult for England fans. Victor
Hugo Morales greets Maradona's second goal in Argentina's World
Cup quarter-final game against England, 1986; quoted in the
Observer Sport Monthly, February 2005.

Danny Mills

Asking Mills to change would be like asking Roy
Keane to become a pussycat.

Steve McLaren, quoted in the *Guardian Guide to The Season 04/05*.

Gary Neville

- The musketeer-style bumfluff appeared
  just days after David's.
- Makes the right back slot on the
  Uglyfootballers.com team.

Two of the '10 things we love about ... Gary Neville', in the *Observer Sport Monthly*, 3 October 2004.

Who hasn't wanted to taunt prissy footballing shop steward Gary Neville mercilessly at some point?

John Aizlewood on Patrick Vieira's taunting of Neville in the Highbury tunnel (*see* Patrick Vieira, page 66); in the *Sunday Times*, 6 February 2005.

English football's answer to Arthur Scargill.

Ken Dyer in the *Evening Standard*, 31 March 2005.

Phil Neville

In his spare time, Gary Neville runs a soccer school in Malta … Rumours that brother Phil has applied to attend remain unconfirmed.

From the *Guardian Guide to The Season 04/05*.

Neville, Neville…

Neville Neville, Their future's immense,
Neville Neville, They play in defence,
Neville Neville, Like Jacko they're bad,
Neville Neville, Is the name of their dad.

A vocal tribute to the Neville brothers, to the tune of David Bowie's 'Rebel, Rebel'.

Michael Owen

This man – what's his name? – the number 10, the small one who doesn't play in the Real Madrid first team – said that if Poland beat Azerbaijan 8–0, England should score at least eight and he'd score five of them … Who is Michael Owen anyway? What has he ever won in football? He plays for Real Madrid but he is always on the bench. I have a history in football, but what is the history of this guy, this midget? He ought to clean his tongue and wash the boots of David Beckham as they are so wet tonight. He didn't score one. Sven-Göran Eriksson is a good man, he should teach him to respect everyone. Who is he anyway? Who is he? … He's a midget and I am not prepared to discuss him any longer.

Azerbaijan manager and former Brazilian World Cup star Carlos Alberto launches an extraordinary attack on Michael Owen, whom he mistakenly believed to have claimed he would score five goals against Azerbaijan in England's World Cup qualifier at St James's Park, 30 March 2005.

Commenting on Owen's performance as a pundit on ITV's coverage of the second leg of the Liverpool v. Chelsea Champions League semi-final:

Owen appeared to have died in his chair without anyone noticing.

Pete Clark in the *Evening Standard*, 4 May 2005.

Ray Parlour

She's got all your cash!

Perhaps the cruellest chant of the 2005 season: Chelsea fans taunt Parlour after his expensive divorce settlement.

Pelé

Nah, Pelé's the black Rodney Marsh.

Former QPR and England player Rodney Marsh, on being asked what he thought of being referred to as 'the white Pelé'.

Zesh Rehman

Twenty-year-old defender Zesh Rehman has all the qualities required of an England player: he is young, versatile and gifted – and has already broken a metatarsal.

The *Guardian Guide to The Season 04/05* on the Fulham player.

José Antonio Reyes

Reyes was caught up in an unsavoury incident when he was at Seville in 2001. The Spanish FA's disciplinary panel investigated the strange case of Seville midfielder Francisco Gallardo who infringed 'sporting dignity' after he celebrated team-mate Reyes's goal in the 4–0 defeat of Valladolid by nibbling the then teenager's penis.

Andrew Hodgson in the *Evening Standard*, 11 February 2005. Reyes commented: 'I felt a bit of a pinch but I didn't realise what Gallardo had done until I saw the video. The worst thing about it is the teasing I'm going to get from my teammates.' *See also* Arsenal (page 68).

Michael Ricketts

If you look up the word 'lumbering' in the dictionary, there's a picture of him.

The *Guardian Guide to The Season 04/05* on the Leeds United striker.

Jon-Arne Riise

Describing the Norwegian's celebrations after Liverpool's defeat of Chelsea in the second leg of the Champions League semi-final:

… Riise, inspired by the brand-new streak of Britney blonde in his shark-like hairstyle, yanked off not just his shirt, but his shorts, forgetting the golden rule that you should never wear your old grey knickers on a big night out.

Jess Cartner-Morley, 'Liverpool's good hair day', in the *Guardian*, 5 May 2005.

Cristiano Ronaldo

You've bought the wrong Ronaldo.

Chelsea fans taunt Manchester United after the Portuguese Ronaldo shot wide during the Carling Cup semi-final, 26 January 2005.

Wayne Rooney

Last of the back-street footballers.

Everton manager David Moyes, quoted in *The Times*, 2 July 2004.

… when the lad finishes playing he'd better have some savings, because he isn't going to have a second career, is he?

David Mellor, *Evening Standard*, 17 December 2004.

You fat bastard, you fat bastard…

Chanted by Norwich City fans, quoted in the *Sun*, 27 January 2005.

Expletive repeated

... it would be nice if Rooney learned a second word.
Martin Samuel in *The Times*, 8 June 2005. Rooney is
estimated to have used the F-word an average 20 times per
minute during Manchester United's match with Arsenal,
1 February 2005.

A foul-mouthed little oik.
David Mellor in the *Evening Standard*, 11 March 2005.

Don't fancy yours Wayne.
Headline in the *Sun* newspaper, 24 August 2004, accompanying a
picture of a fag-chuffing 'haggard hooker' allegedly visited by Rooney
in Liverpool.

Wayne didn't turn me on at all. He was ugly. He had a face like a smacked arse.
37-year-old prostitute Gina McCarrick opens her heart to the *Sunday Mirror*. Rooney was caught on CCTV outside a Liverpool brothel where he is alleged to have paid McCarrick £50 for sex.

You only score in a brothel.
Welsh fans to Wayne Rooney, quoted on bbc.co.uk, quotes of the week.

Where's your granny gone?
Arsenal fans goad Rooney for his 'nocturnal visits not found in Saga tour brochures' (Henry Winter in the *Daily Telegraph*, 2 February 2005) during Manchester United's combustible encounter with Arsenal.

There goes the neighbourhood. *See* ROONEY, WAYNE.
Headword and cross-reference in William Donaldson and Hermione Eyre, *The Dictionary of National Celebrity* (2005). *See also* Tim Henman (page 280).

Wayne's wines

Apparently Wayne Rooney's girlfriend Colleen is given to knocking back £200 bottles of Cristal … when a bottle or two of Mongolian Spumante would probably tickle their sophisticated palates just as nicely.
David Mellor in the *Evening Standard*, 17 December 2004.

Hugo Sanchez

He is as welcome in Spanish football as a piranha in a bidet.

Jesus Gil, president and owner of Atletico Madrid (*see also* page 139), extends the hand of friendship to the Mexican striker.

Robbie Savage

There's more meat on a toothpick.

Alan Birchenall, Leicester City's PR officer, 2000.

If brains were chocolate, he wouldn't have enough to fill a Smartie.

Alan Birchenall again.

A football ground is the only place where a 40-year old accountant with three children, a tracker mortgage, a Renault Mégane on 0% finance and a rapidly expanding waistline can make obscene gestures at Robbie Savage without anyone thinking it the least bit inappropriate.

Harry Pearson in the *Guardian Guide to The Season 04/05*.

Paul Scholes

Scholes spent less time on the left wing than Tony Blair.

From a review of England's Euro 2004 qualifier against Slovakia, 11 June 2003; on Football365.com.

Philippe Senderos

Ponderos.

Nickname accorded the Swiss centre-half by those who detected in him a certain Tony Adams-ish quality, 2005.

Len Shackleton

Because we play at Wembley stadium, not the London Palladium.

An FA selector explains the omission of the self-styled 'Clown Prince of Football' from an England team during the 1950s.

Lee Sharpe

Happy birthday knob head.

Message on a handmade card sent to Sharpe on his 34th birthday by Jayne Middlemiss when the two appeared on ITV's *Celebrity Love Island*, May 2005.

Alan Shearer

Alan Shearer has done very well for us, considering his age. We have introduced some movement into his game because he has got two good legs now. Last season he played with one leg.
Sir Bobby Robson, quoted on dangerhere.com.

Try asking Alan Shearer about the philosophy of English football and see how far you get. You might as well watch him creosoting his fence.
Martin Kelner in the *Guardian*, 21 March 2005.

A tome so devoid of character you could almost see it turning back into plant life.
The Rough Guide to Cult Football (2003) on Shearer's 1998 autobiography, *My Story So Far*.

Alan Shearer and the raiders of the lost personality.
Headline to a *Guardian* article by Harry Pearson, 23 April 2005.

The Newcastle No. 9's interviews have traditionally been a byword for dullness, the oral equivalent of an oatmeal carpet-tile. The sheet metal worker's son from Gosforth has set new standards in the field.
Harry Pearson.

textual intercourse

F****** goodie two-shoes.
Craig Bellamy texts Alan Shearer, quoted in the *Evening Standard*, 11 February 2005.

Your legs have gone. You're too old. You're too slow. You couldn't even kiss my arse.
Bellamy texts Shearer, quoted in the *Independent on Sunday*, 16 May 2005. Shearer replied that if Bellamy ever set foot in Newcastle again, he would 'knock his block off'.

Gary Lineker was an episode of *Desperate Housewives* compared with Shearer.
Harry Pearson. 'It is hard to imagine nowadays that there was once a time when we derided his predecessor as England's premier marksman for being "boring".'

Teddy Sheringham

When I joined, he came walking down the corridor and said 'Ah, you must be Edward Sheringham.' I told him I was, but that I preferred to be called Teddy. He said 'OK, welcome to the club, Edward.'
Teddy Sheringham remembers his first meeting with Brian Clough at Nottingham Forest.

Teddy has lost the yard of pace he never had.
Tony Cascarino on his former strike partner in the twilight of his playing career, 2005.

Peter Shilton

The Thermos-head [Peter Shilton] got cross because of my hand-goal. What about the other one, Shilton, didn't you see that one? He didn't invite me to his testimonial ... oh, my heart bleeds! How many people go to a goalkeeper's testimonial anyway? A goalkeeper's!
Diego Maradona in his autobiography *El Diego* (2004). *See also* Diego Maradona (page 49).

Daniel Shittu

See Doudou Ebeu Mbombo (page 36).

Phil Stant

A forward whose name, perhaps not unfittingly, sounded like a type of bonding solution you'd buy from the Screwfix catalogue.
Harry Pearson on the former Fulham forward; in the *Guardian*, 31 May 2005.

The Animal XI
a footballing menagerie

Faustino Asprilla	=	the Gazelle
Winston Bogarde	=	the Magpie
Emilio Butragueño	=	the Vulture
Jack Charlton	=	the Giraffe
Edgar Davids	=	the Pit Bull
Shaun Goater	=	the Goat
Nkwankwo Kanu	=	the Snake
Oleg Luzhny	=	the Horse
Jesper Olsen	=	the Flea
Frank Rijkaard	=	the Llama
Marco van Basten	=	the Dutch Swan

Peter Storey

He was Del Boy before Del Boy was invented.

The Rough Guide to Cult Football (2003) on the former Arsenal midfielder. After leaving the Gunners, Storey embarked on an exotic criminal career that included running the Calypso Massage Parlour in London's East End.

Mickey Thomas

Mickey was caught *in flagrante* with an old sweetheart, now married to someone else. Her husband's associates stabbed him a dozen times in the buttocks with a screwdriver, later leading to gags about Thomas being lucky to escape without brain damage. Slipping in and out of consciousness, Thomas could recall his assailants debating whether or not to 'cut his dick off'.

The Rough Guide to Cult Football (2003) on the boozy former Manchester United and Chelsea player. *See also* Football and women (page 142).

Francesco Totti

I'm not an intellectual, but Totti's on another level completely. If I spoke to him about the Middle East, he'd probably think I was talking about an area of the football pitch.

Paolo di Canio of Lazio mocks Totti of Roma; quoted by Rob Hughes in the *International Herald Tribune*, 12 January 2005.

Djimi Traore

Bambi trying to impersonate Beckenbauer.

Henry Winter on the own goal by Traore that helped Burnley knock Liverpool out of the FA Cup, January 2005; in the *Daily Telegraph*, 17 May 2005.

Pierre van Hooijdonk

When you're dealing with someone like that, who's basically mad, then you've got a problem.
Former Nottingham Forest manager Dave Bassett on BBC Radio Five Live, 28 January 2005.

Ruud van Nistelrooy

Like a lot of Dutch players there is a darker side to him … On one side he's a brilliant footballer, on the other a little bit dirty, like a lot of us.
Dennis Bergkamp on his compatriot, quoted by Steve Stammers in the *Evening Standard*, 1 February 2005.

Patrick Vieira

La Grande Saucisse (French, 'The big sausage').
Nickname accorded the well-endowed Frenchman for his 'gift from God'.

If you love Senegal so much, why don't you play for them?

Roy Keane to Vieira in the tunnel at Highbury before Manchester United's 4–2 victory over Arsenal, 1 February 2005; quoted by Michael Walker in the *Guardian*, 17 May 2005. The Irishman had emerged from the dressing-room and accused Vieira of intimidating Gary Neville. Vieira did not respond to Keane's taunt at the time, but later remarked: 'For someone who leaves his team in the World Cup, I think he should keep this kind of remark to himself.' (Vieira, who moved to Paris from Senegal when he was eight and, as at May 2005, has played 79 times for France, carries out charity work in his native country.)

Des Walker

He's old, and he shits himself...

To the tune of the Pet Shop Boys' 'Go West', Derby County fans salute the former Nottingham Forest and England defender.

Dwight Yorke

Dwight Yorke, wherever he may be, He is the King of Pornography...

Sung by Manchester United fans to the tune of 'Lord of the Dance'.

● FOOTBALL CLUBS

Arsenal

The first match to be broadcast on British
television was Arsenal v. Everton on 29 August
1936, so the traditional cry of 'Not Arsenal again!'
is older than you thought.
The Rough Guide to Cult Football (2003).

One-nil down, Two-nil up,
Michael Owen won the cup,
A world-class paddy pass gave the lad the ball,
Poor old Arsenal won fuck all.
To the tune of 'Nick Nack Paddy Whack', Liverpool fans celebate their
2–1 defeat of Arsenal in the 2001 FA Cup final. The pass referred to
was by the Irish-sounding (but English) Danny Murphy.

The Italian Job III – Inter Blow Arsenal's Bloody
Doors Off!
Headline in the *Mirror* after Arsenal lost 3–0 to Inter Milan in the
group stage of the UEFA Champions League, September 2003.

All I can say is this. It is just the sort of result you expect when you import a load of posturing French ponces wearing gloves.

Matthew Norman on Arsenals's new 'redcurrant' strip, in the *Evening Standard*, 24 January 2005. The new shirts, to be worn at home games during the 2005–2006 season, replicate those worn in Arsenal's first season at Highbury in 1913.

I wish I was playing for Real Madrid. If I'm not, I'm going to have to go on playing with some bad people. I'm sure there are none in the Real dressing-room.

Little José Antonio Reyes imagines how wonderful life would be with David, Roberto and Zinédine. Arsenal's Spanish forward had been duped into disparaging his team-mates by a hoaxer on a Spanish radio station claiming to be Real Madrid's sporting director Emilio Butragueno; quoted in the *Evening Standard*, 11 February 2005.

Aston Villa

Show me a dressing-room full of nice, polite players and I'll show you a dressing-room full of losers. The Aston Villa squad under Josef Venglos were a great bunch. No cliques, no arguments, no enemies, no trophies.

Tony Cascarino in *The Times*, 4 April 2005.

Atletico Madrid

There's too many passengers in the team. They're not going to laugh at the shirt any longer. Carreras, Santi and Otero are no good. They can die ... I mean it, some of the players don't deserve to live ... and anyone who doesn't like it can die.

Jesús Gil, president and owner of Atletico Madrid (and a man jailed in 1969 for constructing a building whose collapse killed 58 people), launches into a career-ending rant live on Spanish radio, February 2003. When the presenter suggested he calm down a little (Gil had recently had coronary bypass surgery), Gil retorted: 'I'm sick of people telling me to relax. They can stick my heart up their arses.'

FC Basel

You're not yodelling,
You're not yodelling,
You're not yodelling any more!

Newcastle fans taunt FC Basel fans, to the tune of 'Bread of Heaven'.

Bayern Munich

FC Hollywood.

Nickname applied by the German media to the Bavarian club for its various off-field dramas.

Zieht den Bayern die Lederhosen aus!
('Pull the Bavarians' leather trousers down!')
Torsten Geiling and Niclas Müller, title of a satirical book (2004)
about the Bavarian club.

Birmingham City

You can stick your Jasper Carrott up your arse…
Sung by visiting fans, to the tune of 'She'll Be Coming Round the
Mountain'.

Blackburn

It always seems to be pitch-dark by 3.30 p.m. in
Blackburn. There is no language school, nor is
there a fitness centre. And if you want to go
shopping, there is nothing to buy. When I see the
way people live up here, I realize how lucky I am.
Swiss international Stephane Henchoz reflects on life up North
following his move to Blackburn Rovers, 1999.

Borussia Moenchengladbach

Joey ate the frogs' legs, made the Swiss roll and
now he's munchin' Gladbach.
A famous banner, a homage to the Liverpool player Joey Jones,
waved by Liverpool fans during the 1977 European Cup final.

Brighton

Down with your boyfriend,
You're going down with your boyfriend...

Visiting fans' chant, reflecting Brighton's reputation as a gay centre
(sung to the tune of Los Tres Paraguayos' 1970s hit 'Guantanamera').

Burnley

Your town is twinned with hell,
You're ugly and you smell...

A favourite taunt of visiting Blackburn fans.

Cambridge United

You can stuff your fucking boat race up your arse...

Sung by visiting fans, to the tune of 'She'll Be Coming Round the
Mountain'.

Cardiff City

Always shit on the Welsh side of the bridge...

A favourite with Bristolians, both City and Rovers, sung to the tune of
'Always Look on the Bright Side of Life'. The Welsh response replaces
the word 'Welsh' with 'English'.

Carlisle

Small town in Scotland,
You're just a small town in Scotland…

Sung by rival fans to the tune of Los Tres Paraguayos' 1970s hit
'Guantanamera'.

Celtic

Could ya go a chicken supper, Bobby Sands…

A tasteless and inflammatory chant even by Auld Firm standards.
The allusion is to Bobby Sands, leader of the IRA hunger-strikers in
Northern Ireland's Maze prison, who starved himself to death as a
protest against the loss of special category status in 1981; the tune is
'She'll Be Coming Round the Mountain'.

Well I hope it's multi-storey when you jump…

Same tune; same venom. The second verse continues: 'I hope it's
spiky railings when you land…'

I once met a poor little teuchter,
His face was all battered and torn,
He made me feel sick
So I hit him with a brick,
And now he won't sing any more.

Universal anti-Celtic taunt. A *teuchter* (Gaelic-speaking Highlander) is
a Celtic fan.

A plague on both your houses

Hello, hello how do you do?
We hate the boys in royal blue
We hate the boys in emerald green
So fuck the Pope and fuck the Queen!
A refreshingly non-sectarian approach from supporters of
Glasgow's 'third team', Partick Thistle.

No soap in Glasgow,
There's no soap in Glasgow.
Aberdeen fans taunt Old Firm fans to the tune of Los Tres
Paraguayos' 1970s hit 'Guantanamera'.

Chelsea

When asked if he thought Chelsea would one day replace
Manchester United as England's No. 1 football club:

That's the most stupid question I've heard all year.
Alex Ferguson, January 2005.

Chelsea are the plaything of Roman Abramovich.
If he pulls the plug, it's game over. Until he does
it's spend, spend, spend.
David Mellor in the *Evening Standard*, 4 February 2005.

Chelsea going through is a disaster for football.
And if this team wins the Champions League, it
would make you want to retire.
Barcelona striker Samuel Eto'o after Barcelona's Champions League
defeat at Stamford Bridge; quoted on bbc.co.uk, March 2005.

My arms withered and my body was covered in pus-filled sores, but no matter how bad it got I consoled myself by remembering I wasn't a Chelsea fan.

QPR manager Ian Holloway finds consolation at a time of illness; speaking on ITV, June 2005. *See also* Ollyisms (page 108).

The Politburo used the KGB to achieve their ends … Chelsea are using a chain of banknotes that could stretch from London to Siberia.

Sue Mott in the *Daily Telegraph*, 7 June 2005.

Coventry City

You've lost Ndlovu and Whelan…

To the tune of the Righteous Brothers' 'You've Lost that Loving Feeling', Leeds United fans taunt Coventry City, who had just lost the services of… Ndlovu and Whelan.

Crystal Palace

Crystal Palace go down. It is just what they do.

Matt Scott on the four-times-relegated-from-the-premiership South Londoners; in the *Guardian*, 7 May 2005.

Princess Margaret: Mr Labone, where is Everton?
Brian Labone: In Liverpool, ma'am.
Princess Margaret: We had your first team here last year.

Alleged exchange between royalty and the Everton captain before the 1966 FA Cup final. (Liverpool had defeated Leeds United 2–1 in the 1965 final.)

On hearing the pre-match chanting of the Everton fans:
'Everton, Everton, Everton' – it's a genuinely musical city, isn't it?

Comedian Mel Smith before the 1989 Cup Final between Everton and Liverpool.

Once a blue, always a blue.

Well, only until Alex Ferguson makes your agent an offer he can't refuse. Slogan revealed on Wayne Rooney's vest under his blue Everton shirt during the FA Youth Final in 2002. Rooney joined Manchester United for £20 million in 2004.

You gang of f***ing w**kers.

Gary Neville yells at the Everton family enclosure, April 2005; quoted in the *Observer*, 24 April 2005. In April 2003 Neville had responded to claims that he hated Liverpudlians by saying 'The honest truth is I never said "I hate Scousers". I don't hate anybody.'

Everton have to be the worst team ever to have finished fourth in the Premiership.
Derek 'Robbo' Robson, The Tees Mouth, on bbc.co.uk, May 2005.

Fulham

I'm a Little Cottager.
The unfortunate motto accompanying the image of a smiling house on a baby bib sold in the Fulham club shop.

We all agree, Tesco is better than Harrod's.
Chanted by visiting fans. (Fulham was bought in 1997 by the Harrod's-owning Egyptian entrepreneur Mohamed Fayed.)

Halifax

Does your wife, does your wife,
Does your wife have woolly hair?
Rochdale fans taunt Halifax, to the tune of 'Bread of Heaven'.

Huddersfield

Their sisters are their mothers,
Their fathers are their brothers,
They like to fuck each other –
They're the Hudders family.
Sung by Bradford fans to taunt their neighbours.

Leeds United

To many vocal followers of Leeds United,
'Springtime For Hitler' would be read not as satire,
but as a simple celebration of Nazism. 'Spurs are
on their way to Auschwitz', goes a chant Leeds
sing at White Hart Lane.

Matthew Norman in the *Evening Standard*, 24 January 2005.

Liverpool

You are a Scouser,
An ugly Scouser,
You're only happy
On Giro day,
Your mum's out thieving,
Your dad's drug-dealing,
So please don't take
My hubcaps away.

Sung by opposing fans to the tune of 'You Are My Sunshine'.

Feed the Scousers,
Let them know it's Christmas time…

Sung by Manchester United fans to the tune of 'Feed the World'.

Going to Anfield was like Vietnam.

Former Manchester United manager Ron Atkinson on the stresses
and strains of away games at Anfield in the 1980s.

The ultimate failure of Houllier's time in charge was that a club defined by its dominance in the league championship settled for being an upmarket Tottenham Hotspur.

Martin Samuel in *The Times*, 27 April 2005.

The manner of Liverpool's Champions League semi-final victory was classic Wimbledon – a triumph of hard graft and pragmatic defending over superior quality.

Ouch! Duleep Allirajah, Spiked Online. *See also* Wimbledon (page 95).

On AC Milan's 2005 Champions League final clash with Liverpool:
You've got to feel sorry for a side that gets all the way to the final, only to find, standing alongside them in the tunnel, not one of the best teams on the Continent, but not even the best team in Liverpool.

Giles Smith in *The Times*, 5 May 2005. When they defeated Chelsea to reach the Champions League final, Liverpool stood 33 points behind the newly-crowned premier league champions, occupied fifth position in the premiership, and had 55 points compared with fourth-placed Everton's 58.

Fear and loathing on the M62

A man is walking down a street in the centre of Manchester when he sees a pit-bull terrier attacking an old lady. Fearlessly he wades in and, after receiving many nasty bites, manages to get his hands round the dog's neck and presses his fingers in until the dog chokes and dies.

A journalist happens to be passing and witnesses this act of heroism. He says to the man, 'That was fantastic, I'm going to write that up for the paper. I can just see the headline – "Man U Fan in Heroic Rescue".'

'Sorry, mate, but I'm not a Man U fan.'

'Oh, OK, how about "City Fan Saves Granny's Life".'

'No, I'm not a City fan either. I'm from Liverpool.' The journalist's face falls and he walks away.

The next morning the man picks up the local Manchester paper and reads the headline: 'SCOUSE BASTARD KILLS FAMILY PET.'
Very old joke.

On Liverpool's first-half performance in the Champions League final against AC Milan:

… second-raters, country bumpkins against city slickers.

Simon Barnes in *The Times*, 26 May 2005. Barnes had earlier opined that anyone betting on Liverpool to win 'would be certain to have a serious interest in crop circles, flying pigs, a flat earth, extra-terrestrial landings and the innate goodness of mankind' (*but see* page 86).

Manchester City

In your bitter blue world,
You don't go to Wembley,
You don't win no cups,
You hate Man United,
And hope for fuck-ups,
In your bitter blue world.

Manchester United treat their rivals to a variant of the Spinners' 'In My Liverpool Home'.

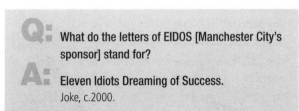

Q: What do the letters of EIDOS [Manchester City's sponsor] stand for?

A: Eleven Idiots Dreaming of Success.

Joke, c.2000.

Joe Royle,
Whatever you may do,
You're going down to division two,
You won't win a cup,
You won't win a shield,
Your next derby is Macclesfield.

Stockport County fans taunt their local rivals as Manchester City are relegated to Division Two at the end of the 1998–9 season; to the tune of 'Lord of the Dance'.

City's going down like a Russian submarine,
A Russian submarine, a Russian submarine.

Manchester United fans enjoy Manchester City's relegation after just one season back in the premiership; to the tune of 'Yellow Submarine'. The 'Russian submarine' is the *Kursk*, lost at sea on 12 August 2000.

Manchester United

So, Arsenal have signed Arsène Wenger because his name sounds a bit like the club. How long before Man United sign Stefan Kuntz?

Frank Skinner.

Next to *Barça*, Manchester United look like Rochdale.

Simon Kuper, *Football Against the Enemy* (1994).

Trouble in the tunnel

Pizzagate.
The inevitable nickname given to an incident in the Old Trafford tunnel following Manchester United's victory over Arsenal, 24 October 2004, which ended Arsenal's 49-game unbeaten league run. Ruud van Nistelrooy was the intended target of a slice of pizza thrown from the Arsenal dressing-room as he argued with Arsène Wenger. The pizza in fact hit Sir Alex Ferguson, 'whose white shirt finished as red as his rage-filled face' (Steve Stammers, *Evening Standard*, 1 February 2005).

A few years ago, the term 'trouble in the tunnel' meant the Circle Line was on the blink again …
Evening Standard, Football Focus, 4 February 2005.

The Battle of the Buffet.
Another nickname applied to the episode.

That's what children do – throw food. That's not fighting. We were real men. We'd have chinned them.
A measured view of Pizzagate from Manchester United legend George Best.

Sign on the door of the away dressing-room at Manchester City for Arsenal's first post-Pizzagate visit:
No soup or pizza allowed inside for safety reasons.
Quoted on bbc.co.uk.

Better dead *and* red

An old man is on his deathbed and hands over his
Manchester City season ticket to his son.
'Here, sell this for me, young 'un, and get us a season
ticket for Old Trafford.' 'But, dad, you cannot be serious!
– You've been a Light Blue supporter all your life!'
'I know that,' says the old man, 'but I'd rather see one of
them bastards go than one of us.'

Originally an Ulster joke of long standing, with Orange and
Republican in place of City and United.

Uwe Rösler's grandad bombed Old Trafford.

Popular Manchester City t-shirt slogan of the mid-1990s, reflecting
a popular nugget of Light Blue folklore. Old Trafford was badly
damaged by German bombs in 1941, and Manchester United were
forced to play home matches at Maine Road for a short period. Rösler
acquired the nickname 'the German bomber' from grateful City fans.
See also Portsmouth (page 89).

A team of overpaid mercenaries.

David Mellor after Manchester United's 2–0 defeat by Norwich at Carrow Road; in the *Evening Standard*, 15 April 2005.

RED AND BURIED
SOLD TRAFFORD

Newspaper headlines following the acquisition of 70% of shares in Manchester United by Malcolm Glazer, owner of the Tampa Bay Buccaneers, May 2005 (*see also* pages 136–137).

United do not need Glazer, they need a goalkeeper.

Henry Winter in the *Daily Telegraph*, 13 May 2005.

AC Milan

Where's the dog track?

Luther Blissett, newly arrived from Watford's Vicarage Road, surveys the San Siro stadium.

We're gonna win 4–3.
With the half-time score at 3–0 in Milan's favour during the 2005
Champions League final in Istanbul, Liverpool fans launch into a
cheekily optimistic refrain. The rest is history; quoted in the
Independent, 26 May 2005.

Dante Alighieri! Spaghetti Bolognese! Cosa Nostra!
Benito Mussolini! Federico Fellini! Luciano
Pavarotti! Donatella Versace! Silvio Berlusconi, can
you hear me? Can you hear me, Silvio? Your boys
took one hell of a beating tonight!!!
A Liverpool fan updates Norwegian commentator Borg Lillelien's
notorious rant (in celebration of Norway's defeat of England in 1981)
to salute Liverpool's Champions League final victory over AC Milan,
25 May 2005. Silvio Berlusconi is, of course, AC Milan's owner.

Monaco

In your Monaco slums,
In your Monaco slums,
You look in the garbage for something to eat,
You find a dead lobster and you think it's a treat.
In your Monaco slums.
Liverpool fans turn an old anti-Scouse favourite against the
supporters of ultra-affluent Monaco.

Motherwell

There were some good things in the game but I can't remember what they were.
Harry Kampman, Motherwell's manager, on his side's 0–0 draw with Kilmarnock, 1998.

If you've got a job to go to, clap your hands...
Dundee fans taunt Motherwell following the closure of the Ravenscraig steelworks in the early 1990s; to the tune of 'She'll Be Coming Round the Mountain'.

Newcastle United

... the worst run since Christopher Biggins sprinted for a bus.
Derek 'Robbo' Robson, The Tees Mouth, on bbc.co.uk, April 2005, as Newcastle's season implodes.

Craig Bellamy and Graeme Souness was never going to work, was it? Princess Anne and Johnny Rotten would have had a better chance of forming a successful partnership than these two.
Football Focus in the *Evening Standard*, 28 January 2005.

Toon Called Malice.
Headline in the *Mirror* as fallout spreads from the Bellamy–Souness spat, January 2005. *See also* page 29.

Norwich City

Norwich … are believed to be considering renaming Carrow Road as Letsby Avenue in honour of their benefactor Delia Smith.

Ian Ridley in the *Observer* has fun at Delia's expense (*see also* page 140).

There's only one Gordon Ramsay…
You only sing when you're cooking…
You're going down with the soufflé…

Assorted taunts for Delia Smith from the West Londoners during Norwich's game with Chelsea, March 2005.

Nottingham Forest

Always shit on the red side of the Trent…

Sung by Derby County fans to the tune of 'Always Look on the Bright Side of Life'.

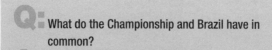

Q: What do the Championship and Brazil have in common?

A: Soon neither of them will have Forest.

When this joke first did the rounds c.1999, it featured the word 'Premiership', rather than 'Championship'.

A Forest fan says to his friend, 'What would you do if you won the lottery?' His friend answers, 'No doubt there, I'd buy a controlling interest in the club.' 'OK,' says his friend, 'but what if you got *four* numbers up?'

Joke c.2004.

Christ Gary, why the effing hell are you going there?

Colleague of Gary Megson on hearing that Megson had accepted the job of manager of Nottingham Forest (then second bottom of the Championship); quoted in the *Guardian*, 23 April 2005.

Portsmouth

Rösler's dad's a German
He wears a German hat
He dropped a bomb on Fratton
And we love him just for that.

Southampton fans taunt Portsmouth to the tune of 'My Old Man's a Dustman', c.2002. *See also* Manchester United (page 84).

You're shit and you smell of fish.

Southampton fans taunt Portsmouth, to the tune of 'Go West'.
A similar chant is directed against supporters of Grimsby Town.

Fear and loathing on the South Coast

Scummers

Portsmouth fans' term of abuse for Southampton and its supporters. According to one theory, this is an acronymic reference to the Southampton Company of Union Men (or South Coast Union Men) – dockers allegedly imported from Southampton to break a Portsmouth dock strike; according to another, it derives from the naval slang word 'scum', a term of abuse for merchant seamen who 'float on the water', and is thus a dismissal by the inhabitants of the historic royal naval station of Portsmouth of the denizens of the merely commercial port of Southampton.

Skates

Southampton fans' term of abuse for Portsmouth and its supporters. In a competition to find an appropriate rebuttal for the term 'Scummer' with which Portsmouth fans have long derided them, Southampton fans chose 'skate' as their preferred term of stigmatization. An established Portsmouth slang word for a sailor, 'skate' appears to have been selected for its degrading sexual associations (it is claimed that sailors on long sea voyages had recourse to skate fish as a means of relieving sexual frustration).

Portsmouth are less 'pomp' and more 'pee' since
Harry Redknapp left.
Matt Hughes and Raoul Simons, Football Focus in the *Evening
Standard*, 25 February 2005. Pompey, however, would have the last
laugh (*see* Southampton, page 92).

Rangers

Michael Fagan shagged your Queen.
Celtic taunt dating from the early 1980s, alluding to an incident in
which Michael Fagan, a vagrant, entered Buckingham Palace and
gained entry to the Queen's bedroom on 9 July 1982.

More Tims than Celtic,
You've got more Tims than Celtic...
Partick Thistle taunt Rangers to the tune of 'Guantanamera'. A 'Tim'
is Glaswegian slang for a Roman Catholic, and the chant pokes fun
at the discomfiture of some Rangers fans with the traditionally
Protestant club's signing of Catholic players.

I'd rather be a Gypsy than a Hun.
Celtic fans respond to Rangers fans racist taunts of 'Lubo's a Gypsy',
directed against Celtic's Slovakian Lubomir Moravcik. 'Hun' is a
nickname originally applied to Rangers fans by English journalists,
and since then taken up by the fans of other Scottish clubs.

Who's the Fenian in the Blue?

Responding to the standard Rangers chant of 'Up to the knees in the Fenians' blood' before kick-off in the final 'Auld Firm' derby of the 2002–2003 season, Celtic fans point out to Rangers fans the presence in the Rangers squad of the Irish-descended Chris Burke.

Real Madrid

Defining the word 'Galactico':

Highly-paid, famous Real Madrid footballer who has lots of skill but no trophies.

Tom Dart in *The Times*, 9 June 2005.

Southampton

 What's the difference between Southampton and a cocktail stick?

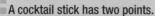 **A cocktail stick has two points.**

A *very* old joke, aired whenever Southampton make one of their traditional bad starts to the season. In 2005 the bad start lasted all season, and culminated in relegation from the premiership.

Sunderland

My magic words at half-time were f***, b*******, b*******, crap and p***-poor.

Sunderland boss Mick McCarthy reveals details of an inspiring team-talk away at QPR, 2 April 2005.

Tottenham Hotspur

You're Spurs, and you know you are!
A notorious taunt, popular with West Ham fans.

My one skin goes over my twoskin,
My twoskin goes over my three,
My threeskin goes over my foreskin,
Oh bring back my foreskin to me.
Bring back, bring back,
Oh bring back my foreskin to me.
A notorious taunt, popular with West Ham fans.

With Arsenal in a gentle decline and Spurs
improving, it is possible to imagine a day when the
clubs are genuine rivals again. This could be as
soon as 2020.
Matthew Norman in the *Evening Standard*, 25 April 2005.

That monument to perpetual chaos known as
Tottenham Hotspur FC.
Matthew Norman in the *Evening Standard*, 31 June 2005.

Walsall

Small town in Poland,
You're just a small town in Poland…
Sung by opposing fans to the tune of 'Guantanamera'.

West Bromwich Albion

Between 1973 and 1988 West Bromwich Albion
FC had the most bizarre sequence of managerial
names in history: Don, Johnny, Ronnie, Ron,
Ronnie, Ron, Johnny, Ron, Ron.

The Rough Guide to Cult Football (2003). The managers in question
were: Don Howe, Johnny Giles, Ronnie Allen, Ron Atkinson, Ronnie
Allen, Ron Wylie, Johnny Giles, Ron Saunders, Ron Atkinson. The
sequence was only broken by the arrival of a Brian (Talbot) in 1988.

West Ham United

Trevor Brooking notes that 'Football at Upton
Park has always been about more than just results,
it's about playing the game the right way, playing
with style and flair.' The obvious rebuttal to this
claim consists of just two words: Julian Dicks.

The Rough Guide to Cult Football (2003).

Describing Upton Park:

You never saw a gloomier, more miserably
embittered den of self-pity.

David Thomas, 'Sack the Fans!' in the *Daily Mail*, 3 March 2005.

Wimbledon

The crazy gang have beaten the culture club.
John Motson on Wimbledon's FA Cup Final defeat of Liverpool, 1988.

No ground no fans,
No ground no fans.
Opposing fans taunt Wimbledon following their move first to Selhurst
Park and then to Milton Keynes, where they metamorphosed into
Milton Keynes Dons.

Wolverhampton Wanderers

Bus stop in Aston,
You're just a bus stop in
Aston...
Anti-Wolves taunt favoured by fans of
other Birmingham clubs, sung to the
tune of 'Guantanamera'.

● MANAGERS AND COACHES
pillocks at the tiller

In football, there is no definite lifespan or time span
for a manager. After a while you start smelling of fish.
QPR manager Ian Holloway after his team's bad start to the
2004–2005 season; quoted on qprnet.com.

Sam Allardyce

[Allardyce is] a man … [Wenger] seems to believe
would taste wine with chewing-gum in his mouth.
Daniel Taylor in the *Guardian*, 11 March 2005.

Martin Allen

Mad Dog.
The Brentford manager's nickname, possibly accorded him for such
behaviour as described below.

I stripped naked and dived in like Mark Spitz.
There was a ruddy great tanker, bigger than this
ground, 100 yards away. I nearly had a heart attack
from that and the freezing water.
Martin Allen on his dip in the icy Solent before his side's FA Cup tie at
Southampton, following a 'dare' from his players.

Whose the fattest bastard in Division One?
It's you Ron Ron Ron, it's you Ron Ron.
West Bromwich Albion fans welcome Big Ron, to the tune of 'Da Doo Ron Ron'.

Well, Clive, it's all about the two M's – movement and positioning.

Ron Atkinson.

Martin O'Neill and John Robertson are out having a pint when three girls approach them.

The first says to O'Neill, 'Give us your autograph,' and she lifts her skirt above her knee and points to her thigh. 'Can you write it here?' she says with a pout.

The next girl also wants his autograph, and she raises her top above her navel and asks him to sign there.

The third girl, not to be outdone, rips off her knickers and points at the desired location. 'Sign here, big boy,' she purrs.

'Sorry,' says O'Neill. 'No can do. Only Ron Atkinson signs twats.'
Joke dating from the 1980s.

Rafael Benitez

Rafael Benitez must be saluted for negotiating his team to victory [in the Champions League] while not quite being able to work out how to win at Selhurst Park.

Richard Williams in the *Guardian*, 27 May 2005.

Benitez had 45 minutes to save himself from being portrayed as Merseyside's answer to Claudio Ranieri.

Mark Pougatch on the Liverpool manager's half-time dilemma in the Champions League final; in *The Times*, 27 May 2005 (*see also* AC Milan, page 86).

– Rafa is the Boss-for us.

– Roman's got his roubles, Glazer's got his dollars, but all we want from Rafa is five Euros.

Two of the many banners on display during Liverpool's incredible victory in the Champions League final in Istanbul, 25 May 2005.

Steve Bruce

I'd rather be Bin Laden than Steve Bruce
I'd rather be Bin Laden than Steve Bruce
I'd rather be Bin Laden
Rather be Bin Laden
I'd rather be Bin Laden than Steve Bruce.

Sung by Crystal Palace fans to the tune of 'She'll Be Coming Round the Mountain', c.2004; taunting the man who left them for Birmingham City.

George Burley

He used to clean my boots.

Preston North End manager Bill Davies recalls his former Motherwell team-mate, about to resign as manager of Derby County; quoted in the *Guardian*, 14 May 2005.

Brian Clough

He was a champagne socialist, a bully, and, on occasions, a vicious drunk.

Martin Samuel, *The Times*, 2 March 2005. *See also* pages 100–101.

Chris Coleman

With his deathly pale skin and lank black hair, Chris Coleman always seems to be about to break into a version of 'Bela Lugosi's Dead'.

The *Guardian Guide to The Season 04/05*.

According to Clough

On the Leeds United manager Don Revie, 1970s:
I just don't like him.

On John Robertson, the Nottingham Forest player who scored the goal that defeated FC Hamburg in the 1980 European Cup final:
A fat dumpy lad who lives out of a frying-pan, but give him a ball and some grass and he becomes Picasso.

He was a very unattractive young man. If I ever felt off-colour I'd sit next to him because compared with [him] I was Errol Flynn.

To his Nottingham Forest players before the 1989 League Cup final:
The only person certain of making the bus to Wembley is Albert Kershore, because he's driving it.
Quoted by Martin Samuel in *The Times*, 2 March 2005.

Responding to a request from Jimmy Hill for an open debate:
No problem. If he can find a ground where he scored a league goal, I'll meet him there.
Quoted by Martin Samuel.

On Kenny Dalglish, 1995:

He wasn't that big, but he had a huge arse. It came down below his knees, and that's where he got his strength from.

On Martin O'Neill (when he was manager of Leicester City):

Anyone who can do anything more than make a jumper in Leicester has got to be a genius.

Quoted by Martin Samuel.

On Roy Keane being sent home from Ireland's 2002 World Cup squad after a four-letter outburst at manager Mick McCarthy:

Oh, I'd have sent him home all right, but I'd have shot him first.

Quoted in Phil Shaw, *The Book of Football Quotations* (2003 edition).

See also Teddy Sheringham (page 61).

Kenny Dalglish

Attending a Dalglish press conference … was akin to walking into a room in which a married couple have just had a major row about sex.

Harry Pearson in the *Guardian*, 23 April 2005.

Ian Dowie

He's ugly as fuck,
But he'll take us up.

Crystal Palace fans salute the rugged features of the man who would indeed take them (briefly) to the premiership.

Sven-Göran Eriksson

He's got a lot of forehead.

Gary Lineker; Quotes of the Year, www.telegraph.co.uk, 30 December 2003.

He was Euro-cool. His heart was Swedish and his head Italian. The mother country was on the rebound from Kevin Keegan, the drama queen and Glenn Hoddle, the religious mystic.

Paul Hayward in the *Daily Telegraph*, 6 August 2004.

Peter Pants.

Sun headline lambasting Eriksson following England's 0–0 draw with the Netherlands, 10 February 2005.

Reacting to Eriksson's bromides in defence of his 4-3-3 system after England's dismal 0–0 draw with the Netherlands:

It's amazing what you can see through his specs. I must get a pair.

Gary Lineker, *Match of the Day*, BBC TV, 9 February 2005. 'It was a good quality game,' Sven insisted. 'You wanted to strangle him,' commented Ian Chadband (*Evening Standard*, 10 February 2005).

Managerial archetypes 1

the continental import

Appearance: Millionaire dentist ... Wears expensively cut business suit, club tie, frown ... While successful, remains inscrutable, urbane and revered both for vast intellect and smouldering charisma. Assumed to understand not only tactics but nutrition, callisthenics, acupuncture and abstract art – all on the basis that it comes from 'abroad'... At the first hint of failure, however, is immediately compared to Inspector Clouseau, Don Quixote, Manuel from *Fawlty Towers* or a member of the French Resistance as portrayed on *'Allo, 'Allo*.

The *Guardian Guide to The Season 04/05* defines the classic European manager.

If Sven-Göran Eriksson was a US president he would be impeached ... if he was a cardinal he would be ordered back to Rome: to a Vatican dungeon.

James Lawson in the *Independent*, 11 February 2005.

Sven was needed to save us from Kevin Keegan, but now we need someone to save us from him ... he's a burnt-out case.

David Mellor in the *Evening Standard*, 11 February 2005.

Sven the seagull.

Headline in the *Evening Standard*, 24 June 2005. During the employment tribunal examining former FA secretary Faria Alam's claim that she was sexually discriminated against by her former employers, FA boss David Davies said: 'I know Sven has a roving eye, he's like a seagull, he can wrap his wings around people.'

Alex Ferguson

Foul-tempered, strawberry-nosed football manager.

William Donaldson, *I'm Leaving You Simon, You Disgust Me* (2003).

Fuck off. I've got a pub to run and goats to feed.

Scottish goalkeeper Andy Goram responds to a phone call from Alex Ferguson, who was looking to sign Goram on loan, March 2001. Goram wrongly assumed that the call was a hoax perpetrated by his former Rangers team-mate Ally McCoist; quoted in the *Evening Standard*, 11 February 2005.

At times he even manages avuncular (albeit like that uncle of yours who is the life and soul of the party until someone knocks over his half-pint of Midland Mild).

The *Guardian Guide to The Season 04/05* on Sir Alex c.2004.

Arsène Wenger's lips are firmly sealed on Sir Alex Ferguson.

Chris Skudder, Sky News.

Describing Ferguson's demeanour after Manchester United's 3–1 end-of-season defeat by premiership champions Chelsea:

Sir Alex Ferguson trudged round [Old Trafford] with the face of a defeated old man.
Adrian Warner in the *Evening Standard*, 13 May 2005.

One Yank and You're Out!
Tabloid headline following Malcolm Glazer's acquisition of Manchester United, May 2005.

Dario Gradi

No-one knows exactly how long Dario has been at Crewe, but the most credible estimate suggests he arrived during the tragically brief reign of Lady Jane Grey.
Matthew Norman in the *Evening Standard*, 9 May 2005.

Glenn Hoddle

Glenda.
Nickname for Hoddle; quoted in the *Independent*, 22 January 2005.

John Hollins

In many ways he's a nice guy. He has a very strong wife. It might have been better if I had made her manager.
Bates on former Chelsea manager John Hollins, May 1994; quoted in the *Independent*, 22 January 2005.

Managerial archetypes 2

the wild-eyed Celt

Appearance: angry Glaswegian publican ... unflinching stare, club blazer, pale furrowed brow ... Nostalgic throwback to simpler era when everybody was called either Ray or Don. Encouraged to throw teacups, have heart-bypass operations and intimidate touchline reporters during terse and threatening post-match interviews ... straight-talking, staring, delivering apoplectic half-time dressing-downs. May seek much publicized training-ground scuffle with over-the-hill playboy centre forward. Heard to say: 'I took a long hard look in the mirror this morning and I didn't like what I saw.'
The *Guardian Guide to The Season 04/05* defines the archetypal Scottish manager.

On a touchline set-to between Everton's David Moyes and Alex Ferguson:
[It] wouldn't have been out of place on Sauchiehall Street.
Derek 'Robbo' Robson, The Tees Mouth, bbc.co.uk, May 2005.

Ollyisms the wit and wisdom of Ian Holloway

When asked how much he earned as a player compared to
Wayne Rooney:
Not enough to go to brothels.

On his team's performance in a pre-season friendly:
**When you play with wingers you look a bit like a taxi
with both doors open, anyone can get in or out.**

Commenting on a poor run of form for QPR:
**Right now, everything is going wrong for me – if I fell in
a barrel of boobs, I'd come out sucking my thumb.**

On a reporter who claimed that QPR were planning to sell
Daniel Shittu in the summer of 2005:
**Whoever that was, I'd like to pull his pants down and slap
him on the arse like I used to do to my kids. Apparently
I'm not allowed to do that any more otherwise I'll have
the health and safety on to me giving it the old hello.**

On the physical appearance of the current QPR squad:
**My lot are the ugliest team ever to have worn the blue
and white hoops – we certainly don't sell many
calendars! In my playing days we had some right good
looking bastards. But this lot are the worst I have ever
seen! They all look like dogs.**

Gerard Houllier

When asked to name his choice for Lyon's next manager:

Anyone but Houllier.

Ex-Arsenal forward Sylvain Wiltord, now a Lyon player; quoted in
The Times, 31 May 2005. Shortly afterwards the club appointed…
Gerard Houllier.

Mick McCarthy

I don't rate you as a manager and I don't rate you
as a person.

Roy Keane to McCarthy at the Irish training camp at Saipan, World
Cup 2002.

Steve McClaren

The run of unusual managerial decisions continues
with Steve McClaren given a written warning for
'looking like a bus driver'.

'What won't happen this week', in the *Guardian*, 16 May 2005.

Jan Molby

Have you ever, have you ever,
Have you ever seen your feet?

To the tune of 'Bread of heaven', Doncaster Rovers fans welcome the
well-proportioned former Liverpool player and Kidderminster manager.

What not to wear

Describing former Manchester City manager Kevin Keegan:

A black polo neck tucked into navy slacks on a no-longer-buff frame? The pocket crest? The belt that is neither thin nor fat enough to be any good? Involuntary shudder of distaste.

Polly Vernon in the *Observer Sport Monthly*, February 2005.

Describing Arsenal manager Arsène Wenger:

You expect more from a Frenchman. Little flourishes of colour, a well judged accessory to eliminate a hint of blandness and absolutely an awareness that you do not mix brogues and sharp creased trousers with a zip-thru anorak. *Jamais!* A lifetime of football has addled his Gallic aesthetic.

Polly Vernon, February 2005.

Describing Barcelona's Dutch coach Frank Rijkaard:

Rijkaard takes the safe continental leisurewear route. He has, however, retained his hairstyle, the one which looks like squid-ink pasta dumped unceremoniously on the plate.

Pete Clark in the *Evening Standard*, 9 March 2005. *See also* The Animal XI (page 63).

Describing former Luton manager David Pleat:

Everyone knows what salvation looks like: it wears a beige suit and a pair of off-white slip-ons.

Kevin McCarra in the *Guardian*, 7 June 2005; recalling Pleat's sartorially challenged jig of triumph at Maine Road in 1983, after Luton's 1–0 victory over Manchester City ensured their survival in the old First Division.

See also Fake tan, Matalan man? (page 124).

José Mourinho

See pages 123–126.

David Moyes

The Moyessiah.
Nickname accorded the Everton manager (a committed Christian) by grateful Evertonians for resurrecting their dreams of glory.

Bob Paisley

I never wanted this bloody job. But it looks like you're stuck with me.
Motivational words to the Liverpool players from Bill Shankly's managerial successor, 1974. The inarticulate Paisley gained the nickname 'Dougie Doins' from his players for his habit of referring to opposing players as 'doins', rather than by their real names.

Stuart Pearce

The referee was not impressed when Pearce went for what is known as a 'Radcliffe' mid-game.
In the *Guardian*, 16 May 2005.

Managerial archetypes 3

the tracksuited Englishman

Appearance: evangelical travelling salesman, padded jacket, eager expression, glasses … known for his introduction of 'new ideas' … spends evenings poring over complex computer models and advanced psychology course in 12 leatherette volumes bought from late-night infomercial.

The *Guardian Guide to The Season 04/05* defines the archetypal English manager.

David Platt

He bought three Italians – one was older than me, one was slower and the third had a heart the size of a peanut.

Former Nottingham Forest star Larry Lloyd on former manager Platt, quoted on bbc.co.uk.

Harry Redknapp

Harry Redknapp lookalike requires cash for corrective surgery to avoid Bagpuss jibes.

Advertisement in *Private Eye*, 1999.

... it would be a blessing for Harry Redknapp to leave football for his true calling. No-one else alive could play an Ugly Sister without make-up, and denying him his pantomime destiny seems needlessly vindictive.

Matthew Norman, as relegation beckons for Southampton at the end of the 2005 season; in the *Evening Standard*, 9 May 2005.

I'm as mad as a box of lights, me.

Redknapp on Redknapp, quoted by Matt Lawton in the *Daily Mail*, 2005.

Peter Reid

In the town of Sunderland,
Lived a man called Peter Reid.
And he had a monkey's heed,
He peeled bananas with his feet.
Peter Reid's got a fucking monkey's heed,
A fucking monkey's heed, a fucking monkey's heed!

Sung, to the tune of 'Yellow Submarine', by Middlesbrough and Newcastle fans when Reid was Sunderland manager.

Sir Bobby Robson

Sir Bobby continues to show. A wonder. Ful ability to. Cut up. His sentences into. Bite-size. Pieces. While saying things. Like. 'We worked. Our stocking tops. Off today.'

From the *Guardian Guide to The Season 04/05*.

Sir Bobby's finest Geordie gibberish

We can't replace Gary Speed. Where do you get an experienced player like him with a left foot and a head?

No team won anything without a dodgy keeper.

The first ninety minutes of a football match are the most important.

Well, we got nine and you can't score more than that.

Anything from 1–0 to 2–0 would be a nice result.

We are all in the same bucket.

I've had to come out of the dressing-room because I don't want to get too excited.

We've dropped two points against Ipswich and I mean that sincerely.

Some of the goals were good, some of the goals were sceptical.

I'd say he's the best in Europe, if you put me on the fence.

We're flying on Concorde. That'll shorten the distance. That's self-explanatory.

A selection of regrettable Robsonian utterances; quoted on dangerhere.com.

Vexing Sir Alf

Alf Ramsey: It's really important that you work hard for each other – you Rodney, in particular. I've told you before that when you play for England you have to work harder. In the first 45 minutes I'll be watching, and if you don't, I'm going to pull you off at half-time.

Rodney Marsh: Christ! All we get at Manchester City is a cup of tea and an orange!

Twenty-two years before the notorious 'toon army' gag (*see* David Beckham, page 24), Rodney Marsh brings his England career to a premature end, January 1973; quoted in 'Confessions of a joker', interview with Paul Kimmage in the *Sunday Times*, 8 May 2005.

Jacques Santini

Every inch the Gallic sophisticate even if he does have more than a passing resemblance to Marty Feldman in *Beau Geste*.

The *Guardian Guide to The Season 04/05,* during the Frenchman's brief spell as Spurs' manager.

Graeme Souness

Graeme Souness does not have a moustache, but he has, by his own admission, had a moustache in the past and we believe he has the capacity to produce and deploy a moustache again in the future.

Harry Pearson imagines George W. Bush's reaction to Graeme Souness's lack of facial hair, c.2004–5; in the *Guardian*, 29 January 2005.

Nobody blows a gasket quite like Graeme

You'd might as well put Bez in charge of the Priory.
Matthew Norman on Newcastle United's appointment of Souness as manager; in the *Evening Standard*, 31 January 2005.

"According to witnesses," … a police spokesman explains, "Mr Souness entered an empty room and seconds later a fight broke out."
'What won't happen this week'; in the *Guardian*, 14 February 2005.

A man capable of destroying the mirror because he didnae like the way the face in it was looking at him.
Matthew Norman in the *Evening Standard*, 4 April 2005.

Gordon Strachan

After Strachan had allegedly poked fun at his weight:

At least I can go on a diet. What is he going to do about the colour of his hair and his silly voice?
Colin McBride, manager of Thurrock; quoted on bbc.co.uk.

Reporter: You don't take losing lightly, do you Gordon?
Strachan: I don't take stupid comments lightly, either.

Graham Taylor

Taylor is a turnip, he's got a turnip's head,
He took a job at Villa, he must have been brain-dead.
Do I not like this? Do I not like that?
Everyone in England knows that he's a fucking twat.
West Bromwich Albion fans welcome Taylor, to the tune of 'My Old Man's a Dustman'.

Bursting into *Raining in My Heart* – 'Oh, misery, misery', Taylor sung to a room of mortified sports writers – [he] convinced the nation that not only were England still going out of the [1994] World Cup, but they were doing so with a pillock at the tiller.

Martin Samuel, 'Time's nearly up, Turnip!' in *The Times*, 29 June 2005.

Some lists are finite, but others are endless: such as the list of reasons why Graham Taylor should never have been appointed England manager.

The Rough Guide to Cult Football (2003).

Neil Warnock

Colin Wanker.

Anagram of the name of the Sheffield United manager.

Arsène Wenger

The once coolly cerebral Arsenal boss is becoming a gibbering wreck, seeing conspiracies at every turn.

David Mellor on the effect on Wenger of his row with Sir Alex Ferguson; in the *Evening Standard*, 4 February 2005.

Fergie and Arsène

the two mad uncles in the attic

It's wrong the league programme is extended so Man
United can rest up and win everything.
Wenger on Alex Ferguson, April 1997.

He's a novice and should keep his opinions to Japanese
football.
Alex Ferguson on Wenger (former manager of Nagoya
Grampus Eight), April 1997.

They are scrappers who rely on belligerence: we are
the better team.
Ferguson on Wenger's Arsenal, May 2002, after Arsenal's
league and cup double; quoted in the *Mirror*, 1 February
2005.

Old vinegar face.
Alex Ferguson describes the Arsenal manager; quoted in the
Observer, 8 May 2005.

Like a ruptured chicken.
Ferguson's descripton of Wenger's behaviour in the
technical area; quoted in the *Observer*, 8 May 2005.

The two mad uncles in the attic.
Matthew Norman in the *Evening Standard*, 7 March 2005.

After Arsenal's 4–2 defeat by Manchester United at Highbury, 1 February 2005:

With Chelsea outstripping the pair of them, last night's affair felt as peculiar as a third-place play-off being turned into World War III. It was as if two wounded old stags were still locking horns with barmy ferocity in their own private war, quite oblivious to how the preening young buck down by the bridge had already usurped their rutting rights.

Ian Chadband in the *Evening Standard*.

The gospel according to Arsène Wenger: even if your player brings down an opponent by whipping out a double-barrelled shotgun and and blowing off both his kneecaps, offer no public chastisement.
Brian Viner in the *Independent*, 19 February 2005.

See also What not to wear – managerial special (page 111).

Nigel Worthington

Nigel Worthington is … sounding more and more like Roy Walker off *Catchphrase*.
Derek 'Robbo' Robson, The Tees Mouth, on bbc.co.uk, April 2005.

● JOSÉ MOURINHO
the ego has landed

José on José:
The Special One
The Portuguese Man of War.

The press on José, 2004–2005:
… the little dictator of Stamford Bridge …
… the gobby Portugeezer …
… the puckish Portuguese …
… Beefcake à la Portuguaise …
… sulky charisma …

The Portuguese professor on José:
The ultimate postmodern soccer
coach … Mourinho is the most
natural genius I've met in my
entire life … [he] spends his
time reading contemporary
European philosophy … Karl
Popper, Edgar Morin and
Thomas Kuhn.
Professor Manuel Sergio, former professor
of philosophy, University of Lisbon.

Fake tan, Matalan man?

That coat's from Matalan.
Manchester City fans taunt the stylish Chelsea manager,
quoted in the *Guardian*, 7 February 2005. The trenchcoat
in question is in fact Armani, and costs around £1200;
Burberry and Prada are other brands apparently favoured
by Mourinho and his wife, who bank at Coutt's, where a
disposable income of £500,000 is the minimum required to
open an account.

**Mourinho's coat leaves a lot to be desired. It's not well
cut, it's not well fitted, and he should elevate his
standards.**
Andrew Ramroop, managing director of Savile Row tailor
Maurice Sedwell; quoted in the *Guardian*, 6 March 2005.

**The suit is pure stealth wealth, the shirt is a baby blue
and button-down with elegant preppiness, even the
socks have a certain minimalist luxe.**
Polly Vernon gives the Special One the sartorial once-over;
in the *Observer Sport Monthly*, February 2005.

Fake tan, fake tan.
Luis Boa Morte to his compatriot Mourinho during
Fulham's game with Chelsea, 23 April 2005; quoted in the
Evening Standard, 28 April 2005.

In his darker moments he [Ferguson] must surely have been tempted to slap the sarky little sod.

Matt Hughes in the *Evening Standard*, 27 January 2005. By January 2005 Ferguson's Manchester United had yet to defeat Mourinho's Chelsea in five meetings.

This intelligent, witty, charismatic and exceptionally good-looking young pipsqueak.

Marina Hyde in the *Guardian*, 28 February 2005.

It is vital that the government acts now and destroys him in a controlled explosion.

Harry Pearson, 'What won't happen this week', in the *Guardian*, 7 March 2005.

… he always looks bloody miserable, does the Man from Milk Tray.

Derek Robbo Robson, The Tees Mouth, on bbc.co.uk, May 2005.

The man … has the manners of a polecat.

Pete Clark in the *Evening Standard*, 4 May 2005.

[José Mourinho] … recently turned down the post of pope when he heard it was something in the way of an assistant position.

Harry Pearson in the *Guardian*, 31 May 2005.

Fergie and the pipsqueak

I like José, I think he sees himself as the young gunslinger who has come into town to challenge the sheriff who has been around for a while.

Alex Ferguson on José Mourinho before Chelsea's game with Manchester United at Old Trafford in the Carling Cup semi-final second leg; quoted in the *Guardian*, 27 January 2005. The 'young gunslinger' made his point (Chelsea 2, Manchester United 1).

… He was certainly full of it, calling me Boss and Big Man when we had our post-match drink after the first leg. But it would help if his greetings were accompanied by a decent glass of wine. What he gave me was paint-stripper.

Ferguson on Mourinho before the Carling Cup semi-final second leg with Chelsea.

He is an enemy of football.

Völker Roth, UEFA referees chief; quoted by Matt Lawton in the *Daily Mail*, 17 May 2005.

See also Referees: bug-eyed baldies and preening popinjays (page 35), *and* Fergie and Arsène: the two mad uncles in the attic (page 121).

● MOCKING ALL OVER THE WORLD
the international scene

England

English – you created soccer but we teach you how to play it.

Brazilian fans mock England at the Maracanã stadium in Rio de Janeiro, 1950.

England have been beaten by the Mickey Mouse and Donald Duck team.

The New York press enjoys the USA's 1–0 defeat of England at the 1950 World Cup in Brazil in 'the game that shook the world'. The US team included a number of expatriate Scots.

We'll keep a welcome in the hillsides...

We'll burn all your tables,
We'll burn all your chairs,
We'll burn all your children when sleeping upstairs,
In your holiday homes.

Wrexham fans taunt visiting English clubs, to the tune of the Spinners' 'In My Liverpool Home'.

You take the goalpost, and I'll take the crossbar...

We stole your goalposts
Your lovely goalposts
We stole your goalposts
And your Wembley pitch too
You never knew how much you'd miss them
Till we took your goalposts away.

Sung by Scottish fans to the tune of 'You Are My Sunshine'.
After Scotland's 2–1 victory over England at Wembley in
1977 Scottish fans stormed the pitch, ripped up pieces of
turf as souvenirs and tore down the goalposts.

Apart from Arsenal, Manchester United, Newcastle and Liverpool, the rest of the teams in England play rugby.

Sergei Yuran, Russian international, sees only up-and-unders, 1996.

I wondered why the goalkeepers tried to kick the ball to each other.

Guy Roux, manager of French club Auxerre, on watching English football, 1999.

England model themselves on the Quentin Crisp principle. Crisp it was who said: 'Never keep up with the Joneses. Drag them down to your level.' … England are the Joneses, always dragged down to the level of whomsoever they play.

Simon Barnes in *The Times*, 18 June 2004; following England's 3–1 victory over Switzerland.

Dutch Ado About Nothing.

Headline in the *Sun*, 10 February 2005, following England's dull 0–0 draw in a friendly against the Netherlands.

After England's 4–1 drubbing by Denmark:

We should really apologize for the interlude in what is really important at the moment – the cricket.

Mike Ingham, BBC Radio Five Live, August 2005, when Ashes fever was at its height.

Estonia

Reacting to the non-appearance of Estonia for a World Cup qualifying game, 9 October 1996, after a dispute about the kick-off time:

One team in Tallinn,

There's only one team in Tallinn.

To the tune of Los Tres Paraguayos' 1970s hit 'Guantanamera', Scottish fans entertain themselves in Tallinn.

Germany

Stalingrad.
Tofik Bakhramov, the 'Russian linesman' (he was actually from Azerbaijan) explains exactly why he declared that Geoff Hurst's shot *did* cross the line to give England a 3–2 lead against West Germany in the 1966 World Cup final.

A frankly useless team.
Simon Burnton on Germany's 2002 World Cup team, in 'Euro 2004: The Definitive Guide', the *Guardian*, 7 June 2004.

And that's England's finest victory over the Germans since the war.
John Motson 'mentions the war' following England's 5–1 defeat of Germany, 1 September 2001.

Hungary

Malcolm, it was like playing people from Outer Space.
England defender Syd Owen to Malcolm Allison on playing against Hungary in 1954. The aliens did rather well, beating England 6–3 at Wembley, then 7–1 in Budapest.

Ireland

When asked which part of Ireland he came from:
South London.
Andy Townsend on BBC TV, *A Question of Sport*.

Let's hear it for the England 'B' team.

A member of the England team greets the Republic of Ireland team at Rio de Janeiro airport in the film *Mike Bassett: England Manager* (2001).

Scotland

Shit part of England,
You're just the shit part of England...

Sung by England fans to the tune of Los Tres Paraguayos' 1970s hit 'Guantanamera'. (The same taunt is also directed at Wales and Northern Ireland.)

Cheer up Craigie Brown,
Oh what can I say,
To a sad Scottish bastard,
And a shite football team.

Sung to the tune of 'Daydream Believer'.

The last time a team in Scotland lived up to the fans' expectations was in 1960 when Real Madrid beat Eintracht Frankfurt in Glasgow [in the European Cup Final].

Andy Roxburgh, 1986.

Faroes 1, Fairies 1.

Headline in two Scottish newspapers after the Scots drew their Euro 2000 qualifier.

Anybody who is thinking of applying for the Scotland job in the next eight or nine years should go and get themselves checked out by about 15 psychiatrists.

Martin O'Neill, the Celtic manager, quoted in *The Times*, quotes of the year, 2004.

I am actually sorry for my friend Berti, because the way his players are punishing the ball will give him a gastric ulcer.

Former West German defender Paul Breitner sympathizes with Berti Vogts's problems as Scotland manager; quoted in the *Daily Record*, 9 June 2003.

There is no technical quality at all … [they are] footballing dwarves.

Breitner again, June 2003.

Spain

Disappointment is their speciality.

Kevin McCarra on the perennially underachieving Spaniards; in the *Guardian*, 6 July 2004.

DRINKING CHARDONNAY
WITH TOSSERS
the owners

I have no interest in schmoozing with other
Premiership chairmen. I don't go to football to
drink chardonnay in the boardroom with those
tossers.
Crystal Palace chairman Simon Jordan, quoted on bbc.co.uk.

Director means that there is another person down
the food chain doing all the real work for no credit.
Director means an inflated salary to swan about.
Director is in the way. Director is a pest. And
director does not have half the influence he thinks
he should. Ask Harry Redknapp.
Martin Samuel in *The Times*, 23 June 2005.

Roman Abramovich

Roman's taxes pay my giro.
Liverpudlian banner seen at Anfield during the second leg of the
Liverpool–Chelsea Champions League semi-final, 3 May 2005.

Ken Bates

He resembled an unusually fey 1960s Kings Road hairdresser.

Matthew Norman on the 40-something Ken Bates when he was chairman of Oldham Athletic, c.1976; in the *Evening Standard*, 24 January 2005.

He's not Norman Bates.

James Brown in the *Independent*, 22 January 2005. Brown remarked that 'some Leeds fans are behaving as if Norman Bates has taken control'.

Thoughts of Chairman Bates

After attending a meeting to set up the Premier League:
I'm off back to my pigsty. You meet a better class of person there.

Phone call to Matthew Harding:
Ken Bates here. I understand you're richer than me, so we'd better get together.

On the late Chelsea vice-chairman:
There was only one Matthew Harding and thank God for that. I don't think I could have coped with two.
Quoted in the *Independent*, 22 January 2005.

It's the blackest day. Bates is interested solely in himself. I'd never shake hands with him because I'd be worried I wouldn't get all my fingers back.
John Boocock of the Leeds United Supporters Trust; quoted in the *Independent*, 22 January 2005.

He may be a bastard but at least he's our bastard now.
Leeds fan quoted in the *Independent*, 22 January 2005.

Glazerman

American excess? That'll do nicely!

Billionaire stalker who will not leave United alone.
Headline in the *Independent*, 29 January 2005.

A snake in sheep's clothing.
Judge's description of Malcolm Glazer at the time of
litigation relating to his (failed) attempt to buy the Harley-
Davidson motorcycle manufacturing company; quoted in
The Times, 13 May 2005. Glazer also fought a decade-long
legal battle with his sister over their mother's will.

He's going to die he's going to die,
Malcolm Glazer's going to die,
How I'll kill him I don't know,
Cut him up from head to toe,
All I know is Glazer's going to die.
Manchester United fans protest against Glazer's acquisition
of 70% of shares in Manchester United, 12 May 2005.
Others sang: 'You can stick your fucking dollars up your
arse', while posters proclaimed: 'Glazer see you in hell.' In
Tampa, Florida, where he owns the Tampa Bay Buccaneers,
the gingery Glazer is nicknamed 'the Leprechaun'.

Glazer sees United as a cash dispenser attached to a
dressing room.
Henry Winter in the *Daily Telegraph*, 13 May 2005.

The bizarre-looking man who has just bought United's global brand … is a reclusive figure despised even by members of his own family. 'He's like a machine – money, money, money,' his … sister Jeanette told this newspaper last year.
Matt Lawton in the *Daily Mail*, 13 May 2005.

John McCririck lookalike.
Adrian Warner in the *Evening Standard*, 13 May 2005.

[Glazer's] knowledge of sport is perhaps summed up by the tale of when he got up to cheer a touchdown for Tampa and [Bill Poe] the Mayor [of Tampa] had to whisper in his ear: 'It is not us who have scored.'
Adrian Warner in the *Evening Standard*, 13 May 2005.

If there was an anti-Glazer wristband, would it be ginger?
'Terrace top ten' in *Spin* magazine, July 2005.

Silvio Berlusconi

Imagine a hyper-egotistical Tony Blair cross-bred with Rupert Murdoch and Martin Edwards.
The Rough Guide to Cult Football (2003) on the owner of AC Milan (*see also* page 86).

Mohamed Fayed

Whether by rapping with Ali G, escorting Michael Jackson on to the Fulham pitch … , time and time again he has set out to make an arse of himself in public and time and time again he has succeeded beyond even his own notoriously wild fantasies.
Matthew Norman in the *Evening Standard*, 9 May 2005.

Stan Flashman

A complete and utter shit.
Former Barnet manager Barry Fry on Barnet's owner. Flashman 'sacked' Fry on some 20 occasions, but Fry would simply ignore the sacking and turn up for work the next day as if nothing had happened.

Jesús Gil

The most corrupt, barking despot ever to set foot in a boardroom.

The Rough Guide to Cult Football (2003) on the former president and owner of Atletico Madrid. Gil got through 39 managers in 17 years at the club, including 'Big Ron' Atkinson, who lasted three months. Gil once said of himself: 'I am Jesús Gil not Jesus Christ'. Ron Atkinson nicknamed him 'Mad Max'. *See also* Atletico Madrid (page 69).

Peter Kenyon

... the downy-scalped wad-waver.

Harry Pearson in the *Guardian*, 13 June 2005.

David Sullivan

He didn't know a goal-line from a clothes-line.

Former Birmingham City manager Barry Fry on the club's porn baron owner.

Delia Smith recipe for disaster

Delia Smith, member of the Canaries' board of directors and small-screen celebrity noted for a cookery course that taught a generation of bachelors how to boil a egg.
Kicknrush (French football web site).

Delia Smith's a brilliant cook
She feeds our whole team porridge
She makes a cracking steak au poivre
But that don't rhyme with Norwich!
Sung by Norwich fans to the tune of 'Yankee Doodle Dandy'.

Had a tad too much cooking sherry, have we, Delia?
Headline to an article by Andrew Levy in the *Daily Mail*, 2 March 2005. 'Looking tired and emotional, and apparently "well refreshed"', the TV chef, best-selling author and majority Norwich shareholder had shouted to the crowd at half-time after Norwich threw away a 2–0 lead against Manchester City: 'A message to the best football supporters in the world. We need a 12th man here. Where are you? Where are you? Let's be having you?' She was met by silence from bewildered Norwich fans. Asked whether she had been drinking, Smith replied, 'At half-time I have a row of glasses of water ready for me because I am hoarse. I can tell you on this occasion it was not too much wine … You forget you are on television. We had a two-goal lead and lost it. I was desperate.' Norwich eventually lost the game 3–2.

Delia: passion cake or fruit fool?
Headline in *The Times*, 2 March 2005, referring to the same incident.

The performance certainly evoked a television chef, but it was Keith Floyd who came to mind.
Bill Edgar in *The Times*, 2 March 2005.

How to make yourself a laughing-stock:
> **Ingredients:**
> **11 Canaries**
> **1 Fowler, on fire**
> **Game, well-hung**
> **2 bottles of Wine**
> **Two bottles of Worthington's Bitter**
> **Half-pint Director's Bitter**
> **2 litres of Blood (rushing to the head)**
> **1 turnip**

Ross Anderson's recipe for 'How to make yourself a laughing-stock', in *The Times*, 2 March 2005. 'As to the wine, Château Carrow Road is perfectly acceptable. It should not be a Vin de Table, although Second-bottom de Table helps to concentrate the mind while entertaining visitors.'

What Delia contrived that Norfolk evening was an act of such inspired idiocy that a nation fell in love with her all over again.
Matthew Norman in the *Evening Standard*, 9 May 2005.

● FOOTBALL AND WOMEN
back to the Dark Ages

I'd like to give her one.
Former Chelsea player Mickey Thomas sizes up a girl who wandered past as he was talking to the then Chelsea chairman Ken Bates. She turned out to be Bates's daughter-in-law; quoted in *The Rough Guide to Cult Football* (2003).

The only place for women in football is making the tea at half-time.
Former England player Rodney Marsh, 1997.

Things to shout to a player who is going through a marital break-up: Stand up if you've shagged his wife!
Harry Pearson in the *Guardian Guide to The Season 04/05*.

One night with my wife for a ticket.
Caption accompanying an image of a buxom blonde on a placard carried outside Anfield by a wishful (and ticket-less) fan before Liverpool's Champions League semi-final against Chelsea, 3 May 2005.

Hell hath no fury

... like a footballer's wife

The words carved into the bodywork of Lee Hendrie's £60,000 Jeep-style Porsche Cayenne by his wife Becky when she discovered that the Aston Villa player had a teenage mistress, 2004:

... prick ... wanker ...

Here's Georgie with a few facts and figures. Our facts, her figure.

Erstwhile cutting-edge satirist Sir David Frost introduces Georgie Thompson of Sky Sports News, during Sky One's *The World's Greatest Sporting Legends*, June 2005. Giles Smith (*The Times*, 7 June 2005) was unimpressed: 'No, he really did say that. It was by some measure the crappiest thing that anyone has said on television for years.'

Companies could make use of a sweaty, lovely-looking girl playing on the ground, with the rainy weather. It would sell.

UEFA president Lennart Johansson voices an idea for bringing women's football into the 21st century; quoted on bbc.co.uk.

FA officials gave [Faria Alam] a severe grilling,
which was a relief, because she thought she might
get a roasting.
Mock the Week mocks the FA's inquiry into L'affaire Alam, BBC2,
3 July 2005.

● THE MEDIA
youse are all fucking idiots!

There's a simple recipe about this sports business.
If you're a sporting star, you're a sporting star.
If you don't quite make it, you become a coach.
If you can't coach, you become a journalist. If you
can't spell, you introduce *Grandstand* on a Saturday
afternoon.
Des Lynam, long-serving presenter of *Grandstand* in his pre-ITV days.

He's a great fucking player and youse are all
fucking idiots.
A testy Sir Alex Ferguson tires of press questions about Juan
Sebastián Verón, 2002; quoted by Kevin McCarra in the *Guardian*,
1 March 2005. Ferguson sold the Argentinian a year later.

Adrian Chiles

… genial long-suffering Bunter broadcaster.
Frank Keating in the *Guardian*, 8 June 2005.

Alan Hansen

He looks like a pissed vampire.
Chris Donald, editor of *Viz*, 1994.

Jimmy Hill

Opinion in England is divided over whether Jimmy Hill is an institution or ought to be put in one.
Harry Pearson in the *Guardian*, 31 May 2005, after Hill had told the *Guardian* what he would do if he ran the country. Prominent features of Hill's governmental programme included a ruling oligarchy of business executives and the reimposition of the death penalty.

See also According to Clough (page 100).

Ray Houghton

Sorry, but I've had a really busy day today. I've been playing in a charity golf day to raise money for a boy who was seriously injured in a car accident ... I had to drive like a lunatic to get here.
Ray Houghton on talkSPORT, 2005.

Gary Lineker

Too good to be true.
Alex Ferguson, 1996.

He's a bit of a babe.
Boy George, 2000.

Crisps ... are high in fat, laced with salt, full of calories and about as nutritionally useless as it would be possible to be. Gary, you should hang your head in shame.

Evening Standard, March 2005.

See also Alan Shearer (page 61).

Des Lynam

Had Des been shot by a crazed fan immediately after France '98 ... we would remember him as one of the great sports anchors. Now he is in danger of becoming a hack.

Martin Kelner in the *Guardian*, 18 July 2005.

Ally McCoist

Cackling Scotch soccer twit.

William Donaldson and Hermione Eyre, *The Dictionary of National Celebrity* (2005).

Rodney Marsh

Rodney Nice-but-Stupid Marsh.

Chris Maume in the *Independent*, 29 January 2005; following Marsh's unfortunate 'toon army' gag (*see* page 24).

Jonathan Pearce

It's a rare privilege to hear a man almost have an aneurysm live on air.
The Rough Guide to Cult Football (2003) on Pearce's live-on-radio description of Eric Cantona's kung-fu attack on a Crystal Palace fan, 1995 (*see also* Eric Cantona, page 28).

Peter Schmeichel

... they could put a parking-meter next to Alan Hansen and I'd find it more interesting watching it click round.
Rodney Marsh voices the thoughts of thousands; in the *Sunday Times*, 8 May 2005.

Clive Tyldesley

If ... a picture paints a thousand words, then Tyldesley is always ready to supply those thousand words and then to add two thousand more of his own, just to be on the safe side.
Giles Smith in *The Times*, 5 May 2005.

Barry Venison

Leather cowboy ties, chessboard jackets, completely straight face.
The Rough Guide to Cult Football (2003) on Venison's dress sense.

CRICKET
It's not natural,
is it?

The night sky over the planet Krikkit is the least interesting sight in the entire universe.
Douglas Adams, *Life, the Universe and Everything* (1982). In Adams's fantasy the 'Krikkiters' wage terrible war on the entire Universe and, as a punishment, are sentenced to be sealed in a 'time envelope' within which time passes infinitely slowly until the end of the Universe.

Why should I buy cricket? Nobody watches it.
Greg Dyke as chairman of ITV's Sports Committee, 1988.

This strange urge to wear long white trousers and a multi-coloured cap … well, it's not natural, is it?
Marcus Berkmann, *Rain Men* (1995).

I'll tell you what pressure is. Pressure is a Messerschmitt up your arse. Playing cricket is not.
Former Australian all-rounder and RAF fighter pilot Keith Miller puts the game in perspective.

As boring as fishing.
TV presenter Anneka Rice, c.1998.

Basically, it's just a whole bunch of blokes standing around scratching themselves.
Australian novelist Kathy Lette; quoted in Andrew John and Stephen Blake, *Cricket: it's a Funny Old Game* (2004).

A poof's game.
Kevin McCarra quotes the opinion of his Glaswegian schoolmates; in the *Guardian*, 25 August 2005.

There's nothing like the sound of flesh on leather to get a cricket match going.
Former Australian fast bowler Geoff Lawson, August 2005.

How can you tell your wife you are just popping out to play a match and then not come back for five days?
Liverpool's Spanish manager Rafael Benitez on the mystery that is test cricket; quoted on bbc.co.uk, August 2005.

● AS OBVIOUS AS METAPHYSICAL BIOCHEMISTRY
the view from the USA

… a tedious, class-ridden English anachronism.
The standard US view of cricket, summed up by Ed Smith in *Playing Hard Ball* (2002).

Describing the month of April:
The month cricket players contentedly begin sharpening their stumps.
Ernest Hemingway hints at a shaky grasp of the rules of the game; in the *Toronto Star Weekly*, 1923.

Watching cricket is easy. All anyone needs is a deckchair, a pipe or knitting, and a week off from the office.
Time magazine.

The rules and nuances of cricket are about as obvious as metaphysical biochemistry.
Dan Howley on timesunion.com.

I don't know what these fellows are doing, but whatever they are doing, they sure are doing it well.
US tennis star Pete Sampras watches Brian Lara and Curtly Ambrose at Lord's; quoted in Andrew John and Stephen Blake, *Cricket: it's a Funny Old Game* (2004).

The view from Planet Venus

Why's that guy leaving? He can't just go – is he fed up with it?
Wimbledon ladies singles' champion Venus Williams reacts to the fall of a wicket during a club match.

Describing the difficulties of explaining cricket to Americans:
Sometimes people think it's like polo, played on horseback, and I remember one guy thought it was a game involving insects.
US batsman Clayton Lambert, quoted on cricinfo.com.

It's sort of like a Russian novel.
Steve Weisse, president of the Tri-City Cricket Club of Schenectady, New York state; quoted on timesunion.com.

We wanna see what you *cricketeers* are made of.
Bobby Valentine, manager of the New York Mets to former Kent (now Middlesex) cricketer Ed Smith, February 2002, when Smith trained with the celebrated baseball team; quoted by Smith in *Playing Hard Ball* (2002).

● COUNTY CRICKET
the unwatchable egged on by the unemployable

Estimating the attendance at a county game at Taunton in the 1920s:

I make the crowd 24 – 23 really, because one of 'em's died there overnight.

Tom Young, speaking to R.C. Robertson-Glasgow.

Describing the state of affairs at Gloucestershire county cricket club in the 1920s:

Only two problems with our team – brewer's droop and financial cramp. Apart from that, we ain't bloody good enough.

Charlie Parker, slow bowler, quoted in David Foot, *Cricket's Unholy Trinity*, 1985.

Too much crap cricket on crap wickets.

Australian batsman Tom Moody, for many years a Worcestershire player, on English county cricket; quoted in Andrew John and Stephen Blake, *Cricket: it's a Funny Old Game* (2004).

Watching county cricket is basically urban angling.

Paul Doyle in the *Guardian*, 22 April 2005.

How to recognize a cricket nerd

Alan Bennett glasses. Plastered side parting. Long-serving oily anorak. Carries holdall with scorebook [and] half-eaten Battenberg cake ... Will pointedly applaud even the most minor milestones – i.e. the highest eight-wicket partnership on this ground between two left-handers called Jeff, one of whom has an interest in Norwegian cinema.

'The Ashes 2005', in the *Guardian*, 18 July 2005.

[in major league baseball games] ... they use giant catapults to fire giant hot dogs into the crowd. Catch it and you can eat it ... If someone fired a hot dog at a cricket fan ... while he watched a ... championship match, it might ruin his day. It could knock over his flask of tea, or land on Philip Larkin's collected poems.

Ed Smith compares baseball's razzamatazz with county cricket's quietness, in *Playing Hard Ball* (2002).

Smashes and bashes

Twenty20 cricket

The game is being forced to reinvent itself to cater for those with the attention span of a gnat.
Martin Johnson in the *Daily Telegraph*, 13 June 2005.

Twenty20 is like being at a barbecue at Wayne Rooney's house – refinement is not an issue.
Des Kelly in the *Daily Mail*, 15 June 2005.

… there are men clubbing baby seals on the Alaskan ice right now employing more finesse, subtlety and a wider range of strokes than the average Twenty20 batsman.
Des Kelly.

If it introduces those, um, 'chavs', to the game, then good luck to it, I suppose!
MCC member on Twenty20 cricket; overheard at Lord's, June 2005.

The Ashes in 2½ hours: it has all the dignity of the Monty Python Summarize Proust Competition.
Simon Barnes in *The Times*, 14 June 2005, on the first-ever Twenty20 game between England and Australia, 14 June 2005.

The tough, uncompromising world of Derbyshire cricket

Sports injury of the week comes from the glamorous world of Derbyshire cricket. The all-rounder Graeme Welch missed Thursday's Twenty20 Cup game against Lancashire after being poked in the eye by his young son – who was apparently copying his dad's John Travolta dance moves as they listened to the *Grease* soundtrack in the car.

Duncan Mackay in the *Guardian*, 10 July 2004.

… a lone, sandwich-munching, thermos-wielding octogenarian surrounded by rows of empty seats. That's if the rain hasn't driven him back to the OAP home first.

Lawrence Booth describes the 'crowd' at a typical English county match; in the *Guardian*, 12 April 2005.

It's typical of English cricket. A tree gets in the way for 200 years and, when it falls down, instead of cheering, they plant a new one.

Former Australian fast bowler Dave Gilbert on the planting of a lime tree at Canterbury's cricket ground to replace the famous old one blown down in January 2005; quoted on cricinfo.com, March 2005. One English journalist commented: 'But what do Australians know of cricket?'

● THE PLAYERS
mullet men and peroxide abusers

Cricketer: a creature very nearly as stupid as a dog.
Bernard Levin in *The Times*, 1965.

The only group of employees more right-wing than their employers.
Former Surrey opening batsman Mike Edwards describes the Cricketers' Association, 1990.

Rain Men.
Marcus Berkmann, book title (1995).

Paul Adams

The frog in a blender.
Nickname of the South African leg-spinner for his convoluted bowling action, described by one journalist as 'head down, body side on, left hand trying to scratch his armpit'.

A batsman's lot

We only get one chance, one chance, *one bloody chance…*
Anon. English batsman on the perils of batsmanship; quoted by Ed Smith in *Playing Hard Ball* (2002).

Kabir Ali

He's bowled like a camel and fielded like a drain.
Bob Willis on the performance of England's Kabir Ali in a one-day international against South Africa at Bloemfontein; quoted on cricinfo.com, February 2005.

James Anderson

James Anderson? Ah yes, I remember. Quiet young lad. Always well behaved. Bowls at a single stump in the intervals. Used to swing it, fast and late.
Mike Selvey ponders the Lancashire bowler's decline; in the *Guardian*, 27 January 2005.

When Anderson took the field in a one-day international at
Melbourne in a shirt without a name or number on it:

Hey, Pom, are you too fucking embarrassed to
have your name on your shirt?

Australian barracker, December 2002; quoted by Angus Fraser in
'Fashion victim' in the *Independent*, 17 May 2005.

Michael Atherton

I knew we'd win something now that Atherton's
not in charge.

Taxi-driver to the England captain after England (deprived of the
services of the ailing Atherton) had won the fifth test match (and
series) against South Africa, 1998; quoted in Michael Atherton,
Opening Up (2002). Atherton was returning to Headingley from
hospital where he had had a colonic check-up.

A natural mistimer of the ball.

Atherton's England team-mate Angus Fraser, quoted by Atherton in
the *Sunday Telegraph*, 1998.

Gareth Batty

A fiery redhead trying to escape the body of a
strawberry blond.

'The Ashes 2005', in the *Guardian*, 18 July 2005.

How to sledge...

Gareth Batty

Gilo's No.2? Does that make you the Queen of Spain?
The Wisden Cricketer, 'Ashes 2005'. (Ashley Giles's nickname 'King of Spain' was based on a misprint on the mugs created for his 2004 benefit, which should have read 'King of Spin'.)

Ian Bell

Bisto kid ... flash in pan ... disposable nappies.
'The Ashes 2005', in the *Guardian*, 18 July 2005.

Ian Bell

The future of English batsmanship has the technique of Geoff Boycott, the patience of Mike Atherton – and the face of a ferret.
Anon. Warwickshire member at the time of Bell's maiden test hundred against Bangladesh, June 2005.

Dale Benkenstein

Dibbly-dobbly South African all-rounder with a name like a New York attorney.
'Slogger' ('A sideways glance at cricket') in the *Guardian*, 13 June 2005.

Ian Blackwell

I'm a thick-set guy. I can't get below 16 stone without making myself ill.

The well-built Ian Blackwell; quoted on cricinfo.com.

David Boon

Boon always looked like a smaller, inner layer of a Mervyn Hughes, Russian babuschka doll. Bless.

'Cricket's Moustachioso', in *All Out Cricket*, March 2005.

Allan Border

Responding to a dressing-room chorus of 'bad luck, AB', after a dismissal:

Bad fucking luck. It's not bad luck. I'm playing like a busted arse.

Border himself, quoted by Derek Pringle in the *Daily Telegraph*, 19 July 2005.

Ian Botham

He couldn't bowl a hoop downhill.

Former fast bowler Fred Trueman, 1985. Botham's 383 test wickets remain an England record.

A fat has-been.

Alleged reaction of Dermot Reeve after Botham took his wicket, 1990.

To think that only a few years ago we were talking of him [Andrew Flintoff] as the new Botham. What, the miserable old bloke in the Sky Sports commentary box telling us how much better it was in his day? Freddie isn't the new Botham. Botham is the new Freddie [Trueman].

Marcus Berkmann in the *Wisden Cricketer*, January 2005.

He [Kevin Pietersen] is getting advice on handling the media from Botham, which ... seems to me like hiring Dawn French as a dietician or Matt Lucas as hairstylist.

Mike Selvey in the *Guardian*, 16 April 2005.

Geoff Boycott

... hailed as a cricketing God by his worshippers and a selfish git by his critics.

Aubrey Ganguly and Justyn Barnes, *The Reduced History of Cricket* (2005).

We sometimes argue about the cricketer one would choose to bat for one's life (consensus: Don Bradman for your life, Geoff Boycott for his own).

Matthew Engel in the *Guardian*, 1989.

A bowler's lot

When was the last time a bowler got knighted?

Alec Bedser, England's master seam bowler of the 1940s and 1950s, bemoans the bowler's unglamorous lot. New Zealand's Richard Hadlee would buck the trend in 1990, and Gary Sobers (knighted 1975) was at least an all-rounder. But what price 'Arise, Sir Shane'?

... to the right of Genghis Khan.

Michael Atherton on Boycott's politics; quoted by Leo McKinstry in the *Observer Sport Monthly*, February 2005.

... as Yorkshire as Yorkshire pudding. Cut him and he bleeds batter.

Aubrey Ganguly and Justyn Barnes.

Mike Brearley

Responding to Brearley's request that his Middlesex side be served less substantial lunches and teas:

Tell you what, Michael, I won't tell you how to fockin' bat and you don't tell me how to fockin' cook. All right?

Nancy, Middlesex's Irish tea lady; quoted by Mike Selvey in the *Guardian*, 16 July 2005.

Mark Butcher

Hey man, Graham Thorpe, right?
A Brixton resident greets Mark Butcher. The Surrey and England left-hander confessed he was unsurprised to find that few Afro-Caribbean Londoners knew who he was; *Evening Standard*, February 2005.

… Mark Butcher's physique [is] now officially a Red Cross disaster zone…
'Slogger' ('A sideways glance at cricket') in the *Guardian*, on the injured Surrey left-hander, 13 June 2005.

Shivnarine Chanderpaul

The possessor of the crabbiest technique in world cricket…
Simon Briggs on the gritty West Indian; cricinfo.com, January 2005.

Michael Clarke

Australia's peroxide abuser.
Derek Pringle on the (then) blond-highlighted batsman; in the *Daily Telegraph*, 13 June 2005.

Paul Collingwood

I've got a little bit of ginger hair. That's what I bring to sides.
Collingwood justifies his call-up to England's test squad, July 2005.

Hansie Cronje

Outside the S&M community, few people suffered more for their love of leather than the late Hansie Cronje.
Aubrey Ganguly and Justyn Barnes on the disgraced former South African captain; in *The Reduced History of Cricket* (2005).

Andrew Flintoff

He has a big wrist; he has a big everything.
Michael Vaughan responds to Peter Roebuck's claim that Flintoff 'chucks' his faster ball, by suggesting that Roebuck's doubts were encouraged by Flintoff's prominent wrist action; June 2005.

Freddie Flintoff: that ear stud so isn't you.
'Slogger' ('A sideways glance at cricket') in the *Guardian*, 13 June 2005.

Empties bars faster than Francis Begbie in *Trainspotting*.
'The Ashes 2005', in the *Guardian*, 18 July 2005.

The TNT twins.
Tabloid nickname for the big-hitting Flintoff and Kevin Pietersen, summer 2005.

See also Anagrammatic England (page 217).

He'd give David Boon's 52 cans a real nudge on
the London-to-Melbourne trip.
Flintoff's Lancashire team-mate Stuart Law, August 2005. The
reference is to the chunky Tasmanian's celebrated in-flight drinking
record, set en route to England for the 1989 Ashes tour.

Angus Fraser

I've faced bigger, uglier bowlers than you, mate –
now fuck off and bowl the next one.
Hard-as-nails Australian captain Allan Border to the younger Fraser,
who had sledged him for playing and missing; quoted by Derek
Pringle in the *Daily Telegraph*, 19 July 2005.

His bowling is like shooting down F-16s with
slingshots. Even if they hit, no damage is done.
Like an old horse, he should be put out to pasture.
Former West Indies paceman Colin Croft on Fraser, after England's
defeat by the West Indies in Guyana, 1994.

I never had the feeling that spectators attended
cricket matches to watch me bowl.
An insightful observation from Fraser himself; 'Bore them out – it's
the only way', in *The Wisden Cricketer*, May 2005.

Sourav Ganguly

Lord Snooty, the squire of Snootingham Hall ...
Take your monocle and and frock coat back to the
country estate, and – boy! Here, boy! – enjoy a
mint julep on the house.
Michael Henderson looks forward to the Indian captain's six-match
ban from one-day international cricket; in *The Wisden Cricketer*,
June 2005.

The biggest shit I have ever come across in the game.
Anon. Australian cricketer, quoted by Michael Henderson; 'So long
Sourav, you won't be missed', in *The Wisden Cricketer*, June 2005.

Mike Gatting

How anyone can spin a ball the width of Gatting
boggles the mind.
Martin Johnson in the *Independent*, on Shane Warne's 'ball of the
century' which bowled Mike Gatting in 1993.

Gatting at fine leg – that's a contradiction in terms.
Richie Benaud, Channel 9 commentary, 1995.

Chris Gayle

The technique may be flawed and the footwork
faulty, but he's first choice every time to open for
the World Bling XI.
Anon. cricket journalist on the flamboyant West Indian, April 2005.

Inquiry to a former England and Wales Cricket Board official who had submitted the super-cool West Indian to half an hour's dreary cricketing reminiscence at a social function:

You get much pussy?

Chris Gayle, summer 2004; quoted by Mike Selvey in the *Guardian*, 7 May 2005.

Adam Gilchrist

Beware things that go thump in the whites.
'The Ashes 2005' describes the world's scariest batsman, in the *Guardian*, 18 July 2005.

His appearance suggests the love-child of Martin Clunes and an elf.
Anon. journalist on Australia's pointy-eared batting demon, May 2005.

The human wrecking-ball … guaranteed to liquify the bowels of any bowler in the world at 22 yards.
Angus Fontaine in *Spin* magazine, July 2005. 2005 Ashes series excepted, of course.

How to sledge... Adam Gilchrist

Did you borrow those ears off Andy Caddick?
The Wisden Cricketer, Ashes 2005.

Ashley Giles

Only his mother would describe him as an athlete.
Derek Pringle on the man whose trundling action earned him the nickname 'wheelie-bin'; in the *Daily Telegraph*, 14 June 2005.

Never shall we laugh at him again. Actually that's not quite true. For Ashley Giles is no longer just a joke figure. Now he is a much loved joke figure. And excellent new rhyming slang for haemorrhoids, too.
Marcus Berkmann, the A to Z of 2004 in *The Wisden Cricketer*, January 2005. The much-maligned Giles took 39 wickets in 10 test matches against New Zealand and the West Indies in the summer of 2004.

How to sledge... Ashley Giles

Milk turns quicker than your bowling.
The Wisden Cricketer, 'Ashes 2005'.

… if any of our batsmen get out to Giles in the Tests they should go and hang themselves.
Former Australian swing bowler Terry Alderman in the *Sunday Mirror*, 12 June 2005.

… part Wally Hammond, part sitting duck for stroppy fast bowlers.
Derek Pringle on the pleasures of Giles's batting; in the *Daily Telegraph*, 14 June 2005.

… notable among cricketers for his left-wing politics and interest in modern art.
The *Daily Mail*, 25 August 2005.

Jason Gillespie

Where's your caravan?
England fans barrack the goateed and earringed Gillespie for his gypsy-like appearance, during Australia's 1997 tour of England.

... with his hippie hair and spindly legs he looked ... like an ageing rocker who had lost his way to Glastonbury.

Simon Hughes in the *Daily Telegraph*, 25 June 2005.

Gillespie needs only a trident and forked tail to get paid work as Lucifer's lookalike.

'The Ashes 2005', in the *Guardian*, 18 July 2005.

A 30-year-old in a 36-year-old's body.

Former England captain Bob Willis on the declining Gillespie, August 2005. The out-of-form 'Dizzie' was dropped for the fourth test match.

Graham Gooch

Moustache type: Christmas cracker clip-on meets western gunslinger.

'Cricket's Moustachioso', in *All Out Cricket*, March 2005.

Darren Gough

... a little red-faced fast bowler huffing and puffing into a little red sunset.

David Hopps on Gough in the summer of 2005; in the *Guardian*, 11 July 2005.

Gordon Greenidge

George Dogdinner.
Anagram of the name of the great West Indian opening batsman of the 1970s and 1980s.

Sir Richard Hadlee

Moustache type: World War II spiv.
'Cricket's Moustachioso', in *All Out Cricket*, March 2005.

Steve Harmison

[His] sinister beard [...] would not have disgraced the Sheriff of Nottingham.
Mike Selvey in the *Guardian*, 3 July 2004.

He has ... the goatee from Trinny's and Susannah's worst nightmares.
The *Guardian*, 18 July 2005.

How to sledge... Steve Harmison

EasyJet are having a summer sale.
The Wisden Cricketer, 'Ashes 2005'.

See also Anagrammatic England (page 217).

... you have got to remember he is still as rough as guts.
Richie Benaud, quoted in *The Times*, quotes of the year, 2004.

Grievous Bodily Harmison.
The *Sun* newspaper finds a splendid nickname for Harmison, 2004.

... hopelessly inconsistent
... Can any fast bowler ever have been so richly endowed in terms of physical equipment and yet so poorly endowed with the mental capacity to use it?
Richard Williams in the *Guardian*, 19 January 2005.

He travels about as well as the most unstable real ale.
David Hopps, 'No respite in tour of misery for Harmison', in the *Guardian*, 7 February 2005. Harmison said of his homesickness during England's winter tour of South Africa, 2004–5: 'I think I must be allergic to my passport.'

Matthew Hayden

Buzz Lightyear.
England all-rounder Paul Collingwood's nickname for the strapping Australian opener, after the *Toy Story* animation hunk; quoted in the *Guardian*, 29 June 2005.

How to sledge... Matthew Hayden

Hayden, your casserole tastes like shit!
A spectator at the Sydney Cricket ground gives the thumbs-down to the *Matthew Hayden Cookbook* (2004); quoted in 'Matt's cool dinners', in *The Wisden Cricketer*, May 2005.
The beefy 'Haydos' appears to be a dab hand in the kitchen: according to his publisher's website blurb, 'A recipe for Salt-Crusted Red Emperor comes from a chance meeting on a Sri Lankan beach, and Calypso Crayfish evokes the sun and sand of Antigua.'

The *Matthew Hayden Cookbook* is available from most bad bookshops.
'The Ashes 2005', in the *Guardian*, 18 July 2005.

Off to the stocks with Matthew Hayden, the devout Catholic, if he crosses himself on reaching a century.
Michael Henderson in *The Wisden Cricketer*, May 2005.

He has the forearms, chest and – in a certain light – face of a large gorilla.
'The Ashes 2005', in the *Guardian*, 18 July 2005.

Eric Hollies

What's the matter – don't they bury their dead in
Birmingham?

Warwickshire leg-spinner Eric Hollies, his bowling underused by his
captain in a match during the 1950–51 MCC tour of Australia, is
barracked by Sydney's notorious Hill. Hollies replied, to the delight of
the Hill's denizens: 'No, they stuff 'em and send 'em out to
Australia!'; quoted by Michael Billington in *The Wisden Cricketer*,
June 2005.

Merv Hughes

Describing Hughes's run-up to the wicket:

Reminiscent of a shopping trolley on a cobbled
street.

All Out Cricket magazine, March 2005.

… he would sledge his own mother if he thought it
would help the cause.

Former England fast bowler Gladstone Small; quoted in the *Observer
Sport Monthly*, 5 June 2005.

[Hughes] was all bristle and bullshit and I couldn't
make out what he was saying, except that every
sledge ended with 'arsewipe'.

Michael Atherton, *Opening Up* (2002).

Matthew Hoggard | the Hogwarts Express

Cheeky monkey crossed with lonely cow-herd.
The Wisden Cricketer, 'Ashes 2005'.

[He] bowls with a small blond furry animal attached to his head [and] wears a broad bottom well.
'The Ashes 2005', in the *Guardian*, 18 July 2005.

Hoggard … looks increasingly like Worzel Gummidge.
Mike Dickson in the *Daily Mail*, 27 January 2005.

The Hogwarts Express served up some magic … He stomped the ground like Shrek and made the ball swerve like a demented boomerang.
John Etheredge describes Hoggard's seven-wicket demolition of South Africa in the fourth test match; in the *Sun* newspaper, 18 January 2005.

He's like a net bowler when you compare him to [Glenn] McGrath and [Michael] Kasprowicz.
Former Australian fast bowler Jeff Thomson; quoted on msnfoxsports.com.

The entire notion of 'fusion' cooking belongs to that category of things – along with the England Test bowler Matthew Hoggard and digital radio – that at first appear a complete waste of space, but gradually prove themselves a useful addition to human existence.
Matthew Norman in the *Sunday Telegraph* magazine, May 2005.

Jonathan Agnew has named his latest dog after the fast bowler. Joining labradors Curtly (as in Ambrose) and Klusener (as in Lance) in the Agnew household is Hoggard. England's hero beamed with delight when he found out – and managed to hold the smile when told the dog is a floppy-haired and rather unruly Pekinese.
'The Talk in Cricket' in the *Evening Standard*, 26 May 2005.

… no histrionics, no macho posturing … only a … thoughtful raise of the eyebrows and a rueful grin. Or, if it was particularly close, an agonized gurn.
John Westerby in *The Times*, 23 May 2005, on the typical Hoggard reaction to beating the outside edge.

On Hughes's moustache:

He always appeared to be wearing a tumble-dried
ferret on his top lip.

Rick Broadbent in *The Times*, 18 July 2005.

Nasser Hussain

Useless tosser.

A nickname given to Hussain who at one stage of his captaincy of
England had lost 21 out of 23 tosses (*see also* Michael Vaughan,
page 204).

Enjoy it, Nasser, this is your last Test. We will
never see you again.

Hussain quotes one of Steve Waugh's standard 'sledges'.

We've got a great list of cricketers joining us –
Gary Sobers, Ian Botham, Graham Gooch, Alec
Stewart, Mike Atherton ... Saddam Hussein.

Former England football manager Sir Bobby Robson removes himself
from Nasser's Christmas card list as he promotes Nobok sports
legends, May 2005.

Douglas Jardine

An upper-class gentleman whose expression of utter
disdain made the Medusa look like Hazel Irvine.

Harry Pearson on England's patrician captain in the 1932–3
'Bodyline' series; 'The Ashes 2005', in the *Guardian*, 18 July 2005.

Right, which one of you bastards called this bastard a bastard?

An imagined quotation by an Australian batsman in the 1984 Australian TV mini-series, *Bodyline*. Spoken when Jardine enters the Australian dressing-room to demand an apology after being sworn at by an Australian slip fielder.

Dean Jones

Fine. Let's get a real Australian out here – a Queenslander.

Australian captain Allan Border to Jones during Australia's tied test against India at Madras, 1986–7. The dehydrated, cramp-stricken and exhausted Jones (a Victorian), who had vomited and pissed his pants on his way to a heroic 160 not out, asked his captain (a Queenslander) if he could retire, but received the above response. As *The Wisden Cricketer* commented in an April 2005 survey of the 'eleven toughest cricketers': 'Now that *is* hard.'

Geraint Jones

It was hoped that Geraint Jones would become England's answer to Adam Gilchrist when promoted to opener, but he batted more like Adam Ant.

Paul Newman on Jones's batting in England's one-day series against South Africa, 2004–5; 'Bok to the future', in the *Daily Mail*, 15 February 2005.

How to sledge... Geraint Jones

You wouldn't get in Queensland seconds.
The Wisden Cricketer, 'Ashes 2005', on the Papua New Guinea-born, Australian-raised England wicketkeeper. Rumour has it that Jones left Australia because he was fed up with being called 'Grant'.

When it comes to being a number 7 with a licence to thrill, Jones is very much George Lazenby to Adam Gilchrist's Sean Connery.
Simon Wilde in the *Sunday Times*, 12 June 2005.

Simon Jones

He has the chiselled good looks of an intergalactic starfleet captain.
'The Ashes 2005', in the *Guardian*, 18 July 2005. The strapping paceman appeared naked on the centrefold of *Cosmopolitan* during the 2005 Ashes summer.

Who knows, before the summer is out someone might actually recognize him in Llanelli.
David Hopps hails the Welshman's success with the ball in the 2005 Ashes series; in the *Guardian*, 24 August 2005. Llanelli is a rugby town.

Robert Key — role model for chubbies

Come on lads, he's sweating Big Macs out here.
South African fielder on a youthful and perspiring Key, during the under-19 World Cup, 1998; quoted in the *Daily Telegraph*, 23 July 2004.

The man with the butcher's boy jowls and the contents of a Goodyear factory hanging round his waist is a shining role model for chubbies everywhere.
Matthew Norman. *See also* Stephen Murphy (page 346).

Key is looking increasingly like a Toby jug.
'Slogger' ('A sideways glance at cricket') in the *Guardian*, 6 June 2005.

… last seen disappearing beneath a pile of pies somewhere in the Medway area.
'Slogger' ('A sideways glance at cricket') on the Kent batsman's decreasing chances of filling England's number 3 batting spot; in the *Guardian*, 13 June 2005.

See also Anagrammatic England (page 217).

Gary Kirsten

Tom Cruise.
Nickname given by Shane Warne to the South African opener after Kirsten unwittingly tried to chat up a group of Australian cricketers' wives and girlfriends on South Africa's 1993–4 tour of Australia. Recalling the incident, Kirsten commented: 'That night I had great difficulty sleeping. The abuse I was sure to get on the field the next day chilled me to the bone.'

Justin Langer

Anagram of 'Justin Lee Langer':
Nul genitals! – Jeer!

He has the wild eyes of a sadistic personal trainer.
'The Ashes 2005', in the *Guardian*, 18 July 2005.

When Langer sledged Nasser Hussain after coming on as a substitute fielder in the first test match at Edgbaston in 1997:

I don't mind this lot chirping at me but you're just the fucking bus driver of this team. So you get back on the bus and get ready to drive it back to the hotel this evening.

Nasser Hussain to Langer; quoted in Hussain's autobiography, *Playing with Fire* (2004).

Langer could drink a flute of champagne, ravage a pretty maid, wear a tuxedo and score a hundred before lunch and still be called dour.

Peter Roebuck, quoted by Paul Kimmage in the *Sunday Times*, 17 July 2005.

… [like] a bit of a tit.

Michael Vaughan's description of Langer's losing-the-plot behaviour after the Australian's claim for a catch off a Vaughan cover-drive was turned down by the umpire in the second test at Adelaide, November 2004. Vaughan added: 'He was so red-faced I thought he had turned into something out of a giant packet of matches'; quoted by Paul Kimmage in the *Sunday Times*, 17 July 2005.

Brian Lara

The last emperor of West Indies cricket.

Anon. journalist, April 2004, following Lara's record-breaking 400 not out against England at Antigua.

In Trinidad Brian Lara is the Messiah … To many others elsewhere in the Caribbean, he is … a very naughty boy.

John Stern in 'The life of Brian', cricinfo.com, May 2005.

He has lost 53 of his 115 Tests, and is only one defeat short of joining Alec Stewart as test cricket's greatest loser.

John Stern on a player who has scored 4654 of his 10,818 test runs in losing causes.

Brett Lee

Porn-star looks and wonky radar.

Anon. Australian journalist, spring 2005.

He runs in like a finely tuned athlete, releases the globe like a tightly coiled spring, girls swooning at the sight of his sweeping golden locks – then he gets hit for 20 in an over.

Rob Smyth, '10 Aussies who can help England win the Ashes', in *Spin* magazine, May 2005.

Lee … for some reason reminds me of Tin Tin … he always looks just a little too scrubbed up for a fast bowler.

Mike Selvey in the *Guardian*, 9 July 2005.

Suit you, Brett?

Occupation: Australian Cricketer and Suit Salesman at Barclays Menswear.

Favourite Food: His mum's lasagne.

Favourite music: Ranges from Mozart to AC/DC.

He uses Forever & Avon soaps & shampoos.

Brett's favourite song is 'When You Say Nothing At All' by Ronan Keating.

Brett likes to eat Butter Chicken.

Six things you did not need to know about Brett Lee; from 'The Official Brett Lee website', www.brettlee.net.

Lee has the athleticism of a gymnast, the strength of a rugby player and the backside of a National Express coach driver with a Mr Kipling habit.

'The Ashes 2005', in the *Guardian*, 18 July 2005.

How to sledge... Jon Lewis

We've heard of John Lewis. Expensive and crap at delivering.

The Wisden Cricketer, 'Ashes 2005', on the Gloucestershire seamer.

Dennis Lillee

Hitler, Stalin, Einstein, Dali, Groucho, Lillee. The connection between these names is as plain as the hair on your face: world-beaters wear moustaches.

Angus Fontaine in *Spin* magazine, July 2005.

Martin McCague

Reacting to the presence of the Northern-Irish-born but Australian-raised McCague in England's squad for the 1994–5 Ashes tour down under:

The first-known case of a rat joining a sinking ship.

Anon. Australian.

Craig McDermott

Hey, hey, hey, hey! I'm fucking talking to you. Come here, come here, come here, come here … Do that again and you're on the next plane home, son … What was that? You fucking test me and you'll see.

Australian captain Allan Border, mid-pitch tirade to fast bowler Craig McDermott after McDermott had asked Border if he could change ends; at Taunton during Australia's 1993 Ashes tour of England; quoted on cricinfo.com.

Glenn McGrath

McGrath just chunters away like the worst kind of hectoring mother-in-law. Nag, nag, nag.
Piers Morgan on the relentless accuracy that has brought McGrath more than 500 test wickets; *Observer Sport Monthly*, 5 June 2005.

That Glenn McGrath ... what a bastard.
Cricket nut Sir Mick Jagger on Australia's veteran seamer; quoted on cricinfo.com, August 2005. After England's victory in the second test match over a McGrath-less Australia at Edgbaston, McGrath revised his earlier prediction of a 5–0 Australian series victory, saying: 'It's down to 3–1 at the moment!' *See also* page 224.

Devon Malcolm

Devon Malcolm is the scattergun of test cricket, capable on his worst days of putting the fear of God into short leg ... rather than the batsman. But sometimes, when the force is with him and he puts his contact lenses in the correct eyes, he can be devastating.
Mike Selvey in the *Guardian*, 1995.

Damien Martin

He walks out to bat radiating as much intensity as someone toddling to the newsagent for the Racing Post.
Gideon Haigh, 14 September 2005.

Khaled Mashud

Khaled Mashud – a genuine all-rounder in that he is mediocre at more than one discipline.
Mike Selvey on the Bangladesh player; in the *Guardian*, 17 June 2005.

Muttiah Muralitharan

The game's leading wicket-taker is one of the great masters in Shane Warne, and hard on his heels is a burglar, a thief, a dacoit.
Former Indian spin bowler Bishan Bedi on Muralitharan; quoted on cricinfo.com.

Boy George would be considered straight at the University of Western Australia.
Former Australian leg-spinner Kerry O'Keeffe queries the reliability of tests done on Muralitharan's notoriously bent bowling arm, 2004; quoted on cricinfo.com.

André Nel

Nelly, as I imagine nobody alive would dare call him to his face, must be the most extravagantly psychotic character ever to grace world cricket.
Matthew Norman in the *Evening Standard*, 24 January 2005.

As a fast bowler he looks mediocre, as a sledger he stands alone.
Matthew Norman.

... if ever a man needed a huge spliff before taking to the field, that man is André Nel.
Matthew Norman discovers 'a little bother with marijuana' in the fast bowler's curriculum vitae.

Bling, bullshit and...
a 50-grand ear stud

Pietersen's arrival is causing unease among his fellow-professionals, many of whom regard him as a cocky little pillock.
Matthew Engel on England's new boy Kevin Pietersen, quoted on cricinfo.com.

Pietersen would be deemed brash by a Texan assertiveness coach.

Simon Wilde in the *Sunday Times*, 12 June 2005.

On the South African-born Pietersen's kissing his England badge after scoring his first one-day international century:
It was the kiss of a randy bed-hopper...
Frank Keating in the *Guardian*, 4 February 2005.

Pietersen's technique will make top-class bowlers salivate.
Michael Atherton in the *Sunday Telegraph*, 6 February 2005.

I didn't want Budd then, and I don't want Pietersen now.
Peter Oborne, 'Brilliant, but this batsman doesn't belong to England', in the *Evening Standard*, 7 February 2005. Oborne was comparing two white South Africans who chose to represent Britain. Zola Budd ran for Britain in the women's 3000 metres at the 1984 Olympics.

There are 246 Google entries for "Kevin Pietersen traitor". "Hansie Cronje traitor" brings up only 56.
Tanya Aldred in the *Guardian*, 14 February 2005.

Describing Pietersen's 'dubious accent':
… a frothy cocktail of Bow bells, Sheffield town hall and Durban beach.
Tanya Aldred.

First thing I'm doing when we're out of here is getting him to the barber's, to get that dead mongoose off his head.
Ian Botham (whose management company is looking after Pietersen's affairs) finds a metaphor for Pietersen's two-tone peroxide mohican; quoted in the *Daily Telegraph*, 9 March 2005. Pietersen's mother, Penny, remarked: 'When he asked me what I thought about his hairstyle I said, no matter what happened, a mother would always love her child' (quoted in the *Daily Telegraph*, 28 April 2005).

He's nicknamed me '600', because he wants me to become his 600th test wicket.
Pietersen on his Hampshire captain and new friend Shane Warne; quoted in the *Independent*, 9 May 2005. The unlucky 600th in fact turned out to be Marcus Trescothick.

Australia driven nuts by KP.
Headline in the *Evening Standard*, 12 September 2005, as Pietersen's second innings 158 in the final test ensured England a draw, a 2–1 series victory – and the Ashes.

See also Anagrammatic England (page 217).

Harry Pilling

Bloody hell, Pilling, you're still eight not out in the *Manchester Evening News*!

An Old Trafford member barracks the Lancashire batsman Harry Pilling for slow batting during a match in the 1960s; quoted by Martin Johnson in the *Daily Telegraph*, 13 June 2005.

Ricky Ponting

He walks with the rat-a-tat stride and pained expression of a man in urgent need of the nearest toilet.

'The Ashes 2005', in the *Guardian*, 18 July 2005.

Ponting resembles George W. Bush and leads like him too.

Tim de Lisle in *The Times*, 13 August 2005; Ponting was criticized for his captaincy during the third Ashes test match at Old Trafford, but his match-saving innings of 156 suggests he may be a better batsman than the US president.

Derek Randall

Sorry lads, I'm batting like Wally Hammond, but running like Charlie Chaplin.

Randall to his Nottinghamshire team-mates on returning not out to the dressing-room at the tea break, having run three of them out; quoted in *All Out Cricket* magazine, June 2005.

Rev. David Sheppard

Kid yourself it's a Sunday, Rev., and put your hands together.

Fred Trueman to Sheppard during the 1962–3 MCC tour of Australia, when the future Bishop of Liverpool's catching was a little rusty; quoted by John Woodcock in *The Times*, 8 March 2005.

Gladstone Small

Does he have a brother called 'Disraeli Big'?

Overheard at Lord's, late 1980s. The forename of the near-neckless former England and Warwickshire paceman is a portmanteau of his parent's names, *Glad*ys and *Stan*ley.

Ed Smith

Ed Smith disguised any nerves with such quin-tessentially English charm that one observer wondered whether Hugh Grant had been drafted into the squad.

Richard Hobson in *The Times,* on Smith's first England press conference, summer 2003.

He has been an endless source of amusement, especially for the Yorkshire boys. They have never heard anybody speak before like Ed. At the crease he looks a million dollars, which is probably what he has got tucked away somewhere.

Mark Butcher on his unfeasibly well-spoken new England team-mate, summer 2003, quoted on cricinfo.com.

A cricketer's fan mail

Dear Ed

I can't go on any longer without writing to you. I must say from the outset that I find you impossibly attractive both facially and physically. I have been watching with rapt attention while you have made your debut at Trent Bridge. I must admit at this point, Ed, that I am an older gay man, though all my friends tell me that I am extremely good-looking and youthful in manner. As I live quite locally in Kent, why not pop in if you are ever passing?

From a letter found by Ed Smith on his seat in the England dressing-room, summer 2003; quoted in Ed Smith, *On and Off the Field* (2004).

Said to Smith when he entered the Lancashire dressing-room in search of a can of Coke:

You can fook off, that's what you can do.

Lancashire's Peter Martin; quoted in Ed Smith, *On and Off the Field* (2004).

Graeme Smith

He has no finesse. He merely stands tall and heaves everything in the V between straight and mid-wicket.

David Hopps on South Africa's captain; in the *Guardian*, 10 February 2005.

He has no wit … I don't think he's too intelligent, actually … I know a lot of people who have no time for him, including his own players.

Kevin Pietersen, quoted in the *Independent*, 9 May 2005.

John Snow

… a fast bowler so hot-headed it was a surprise his sun hat never burst into flames.

Harry Pearson on England's fast-bowling hero of the 1970–71 Ashes series; in 'The Ashes 2005', in the *Guardian*, 18 July 2005.

Alec Stewart

... pure Alan Partridge.
Mike Walters on Alec Stewart's public relations at the 1999 World Cup; in the *Mirror*, 1 February 2005.

Andrew Strauss

Lord Brocket.
Strauss's new England team-mate Matthew Hoggard christens the Radley-educated Middlesex opener, summer 2004. Other inevitable Strauss nicknames are Johann and Levi.

Barry Big Pants.
Nickname applied to Strauss by his Middlesex county colleagues in the wake of his success as an England opener, summer 2004.

Andrew Strauss: you look a bit like a chipmunk.
'Slogger' ('A sideways glance at cricket') in the *Guardian*, 13 June 2005.

How to sledge... **Andrew Strauss**

Gonna take guard – or does your butler do that for you?
The Wisden Cricketer, 'Ashes 2005'.

I have got plans for all the guys I bowl to, especially Straussy. I call him the new Daryll. He's the new Cullinan, I reckon.

Shane Warne after the second Ashes test match, August 2005, during which he had taken Strauss's wicket with an extravagant leg-break. The South African batsman Daryll Cullinan was a 1990s victim of Warne's leg-spinning – and sledging – prowess (*see* page 227).

See also Anagrammatic England (page 217).

Andrew Symonds

Responding to the question 'Sex before a game?':

Mate, when you look like me you tend to take it when you can get it.

Symonds, interview with Angus Fontaine in *Spin* magazine, July 2005.

Chris Tavaré

Seagulls were never safer or smugger than when Chris Tavaré was at bat.

Angus Fontaine in *Spin* magazine, July 2005.

Ever wondered why the Australians bat like the hot breath of hell is on their necks? It's because they were young, impressionable kids when the memory of Tavaré's stultifying stone-walling in the 1982–3 Ashes series was tattooed on their brains.

So hell-for-leather modern Australian batsmanship is all Tavaré's fault. Angus Fontaine in *Spin* magazine, July 2005.

Graham Thorpe

… his face looks wary, weary, and his piercing eyes
could … freeze hell over.
Rob Smyth in *The Wisden Cricketer*, June 2005.

The word nurdle could have been invented for
Thorpe.
'The Ashes 2005', in the *Guardian*, 18 July 2005.

After Thorpe had dropped Australian opening batsman Matthew
Elliot in the Headingley test match of 1997:
Congratulations Mr Thorpe. You have just cost us
the Ashes.
England captain Michael Atherton. England and Australia were tied
at 1–1 after three Tests, and Australia had limped to 50 for four in
reply to England's 172. Elliot went on to make 199; quoted in the
Guardian, 3 May 2005.

Advice given to Thorpe, whose fractured little finger had threatened
his participation in England's run-chase in the third test match
against the West Indies, August 2004:
Cut it off, lad – you've got a Test match to win!
Geoffrey Boycott.

On Graham Thorpe's new coaching role with the Australian Pura Cup winners for the 2005–6 season:

Why do we need a Pom to help us out…?

Hard-bitten New South Welshman Steve Waugh; in his *Daily Telegraph* column, May 2005.

Like a many-ringed tree-strump, he's short, ancient and very hard to remove.

'The Ashes 2005', in the *Guardian*, 18 July 2005. On 14 July Thorpe was dropped from the England team for the first test match in place of Kevin Pietersen.

Marcus Trescothick

Banger.

The England opener's former nickname came not from his robust hitting, but from his love of sausages. 'Other nicknames include 'Tres' and 'Tresco'. But never Thick' (the *Guardian*, 18 July 2005).

Describing the Trescothick play-and-miss:

Man-clearing-nettles off-stump waft.

'The Ashes 2005', in the *Guardian*, 18 July 2005.

See also Anagrammatic England (page 217).

How to sledge... Marcus Trescothick

Is that lead in your feet – or are you just pleased to see us?
The Wisden Cricketer, 'Ashes 2005'.

Fred Trueman

People started calling me 'Fiery' because 'Fiery' rhymes with Fred, just as 'Typhoon' rhymes with Tyson.
Trueman, quoted in Andrew John and Stephen Blake, *Cricket: it's a Funny Old Game* (2004).

See also Ian Botham (page 164).

Alex Tudor

The possessor of the spindliest body known to the fast bowling fraternity.
Simon Hughes in *Spin* magazine, May 2005.

Phil Tufnell

On Tufnell's test bowling average of 37 runs per wicket:
Okay, maybe the stats aren't so impressive, but ... Hell, you try to bowl spin when you've got an ex-girlfriend's dad running after you with a brick.
Aubrey Ganguly and Justyn Barnes, *The Reduced History of Cricket* (2005).

 **down down, dumber and down ... under?**

He immersed himself in the music of Status Quo.
A helpful insight, courtesy of Ian Chappell (Jeff Thomson's captain on Australia's 1975 Ashes tour), into the cultural hinterland of a man who once remarked to his Australian team-mates: 'You guys all think I'm a dumb fast bowler.'

Chaminda Vaas

If someone has a cute figure, they are known as having a nice Chaminda.
The former Australian leg-spinner Kerry O'Keeffe on the Sri Lankan fast bowler's contribution to Australian slang; quoted on cricinfo.com.

Michael Vaughan

Once routinely portayed as a pottering country vicar, Vaughan stands accused of arrogance.
David Hopps in the *Guardian*, 31 January 2005. Match referee Clive Lloyd called Vaughan 'rude and dismissive' when the England captain allegedly refused to accept gracefully a punishment that fined him his entire match fee after he criticized the umpires for inconsistency on bad-light decisions in the fourth England v. South Africa test match at the Wanderers, Johannesburg.

In 2003 he was genuinely likeable. Now he is just a genuine *doos*.

Anonymous South African player on the new, tougher Vaughan, January 2005; quoted by David Hopps in the *Guardian*, 31 January 2005. *Doos* is an Afrikaans insult that literally translates as 'box'. South Africa had just lost an enthralling test series to England 2–1.

Vaughan is the worst tosser in cricket.

Piers Morgan alludes to the England captain's habit of losing the toss; in the *Observer Sports Monthly*, 5 June 2005 (*see also* Nasser Hussain, page 180).

Vaughan's inscrutable demeanour has led to some unkind comparisons with Thunderbirds puppets.

'The Ashes 2005', in the *Guardian*, 18 July 2005. Vaughan is nicknamed 'Virgil' for his supposed resemblance to the Thunderbird Virgil Tracy.

See also Anagrammatic England (page 217).

Shane Warne

See pages 206–209.

Shane Watson

A big blonde hulk with highlights … who is scared of ghosts.

Kevin Mitchell in the *Observer*, 26 June 2005. The reference is to Watson's experiences in Lumley Castle, Chester-le-Street, where he was so spooked by the story of the ghost of Lily Lumley that he spent the night on the floor of Brett Lee's room. Bless. *See also* A sledger's dozen (page 230).

Bev Waugh

The mother of all Waughs, Bev gave birth to … Stephen and Mark on June 2, 1965, delivering Australia a combined 19,000 runs, 52 tons, 153 wickets and 293 catches in 296 tests – and world supremacy. Forget Warne to Gatting in '93, this was the delivery of the century.

Angus Fontaine in *Spin* magazine, July 2005.

Steve Waugh

After Waugh – in the space of six minutes – ran out Damien Martyn and trod on his own stumps without scoring in the first match of his last test series (against India at Brisbane):

As far as farewells go, this was like Dame Nellie Melba getting a frog in her throat. Then falling into the orchestra pit.

Trevor Marshallsea in *The Sydney Morning Herald*, December 2003.

● Hornie Warnie
greatest text cricketer of them all

Cool, insouciant and chavish – a football star in cricketing whites.
Simon Hattenstone in the *Guardian*, 19 July 2005.

The Victorian viper.
Nickname accorded Warne for his guile and venom with the ball.

Anagram of 'Shane Keith Warne':
Is heathen wanker.

The Bogan from Black Rock.
Malcolm Conn, 'Cyclone Shane', in *The Australian*, 28 June 2005.
'Bogan' is a slang term meaning 'uncouth person'; Black Rock is the Melbourne seaside suburb where Warne grew up.

How to sledge... Shane Warne

You've got another bald spot coming on, Warney.
The Wisden Cricketer, 'Ashes 2005'.

Responding to the claim that he put on two stone in weight during one summer of league cricket in England:

It's simply not true: I put on close to 3½ stone. I came over 81kg and was just off 100kg when I came back … I drank every night and ate absolute rubbish for six months.
Quoted by Simon Hattenstone.

Always late, badly dressed.
A 'leading sponsor's representative' describes Warne; quoted by Malcolm Conn in *The Australian*, 28 June 2005.

… if not the greatest Test cricketer of all time, then certainly the greatest text cricketer of all time.
Michael Atherton in the *Sunday Telegraph*, 12 June 2005, alluding to Warne's occasional practice of sending lubricious text messages, a penchant believed by some to have cost him the position of Australian test captain.

Cries of 'Bowled, Warnie!' [have] given way to 'Bald, Warnie!'
Simon Wilde in the *Sunday Times*, 17 July 2005. On the eve of the Ashes series, Warne confirmed he had signed up with Advanced Hair Studio (previous clients: Graham Gooch, Austin Healey) to replenish his thinning locks. The press blurb for the treatment stated that it 'should make it easy to bowl a maiden over'. Kevin Pietersen described Warne's hair as 'wearing like a fifth-day wicket' (June 2005).

The first thing he said was: 'How about a foursome?' I thought, who is this creep?

Laura Sayers, friend of a friend of Kevin Pietersen's, meets a decidedly horny Warnie in KP's London flat; quoted by Mike Duffy in the *Sunday Mirror*, 19 June 2005.

He's a bit chubby, but he's quite fit. It was all over very quickly. He wasn't very well endowed. He just wanted to get laid. As soon as it was over, he fell asleep snoring.

What it's like to have sex with the finest leg-spin bowler who ever drew breath; Sayers again, quoted by Mike Duffy.

When hit for four he sounds not dissimilar to Maria Sharapova.

'The Ashes 2005', in the *Guardian*, 18 July 2005.

Michael Jackson is forever 13. Shane Warne is 18.

Peter Roebuck, 'A legend who failed life's tests', in the *Sydney Morning Herald*, 28 June 2005.

My diet is still pizzas, chips, toasted cheese sandwiches and milkshakes. I have the occasional six-week burst where I stick to fruit and cereal: it bloody kills me.

Shane Warne on the not-so-secret ingredients to his success, quoted on cricinfo.com, summer 2005.

It ain't over until the fat man spins.

Australian banner waved during the fifth test match of the 2005 Ashes series, 12 September 2005. Warne took 40 wickets in the series – in a losing cause.

● BEHIND THE SUNGLASSES
the coaches

John Buchanan

A shadowy string-puller best known for baffling his players with the writings of ancient Chinese warlords.

Simon Briggs on the Australian coach, in the *Daily Telegraph*, 6 July 2005. Buchanan quoted *The Art of War*, a treatise by the ancient Chinese warlord Sun Tzu, as an inspiration to the 2001 touring Australians.

[He] put the confusion in Confucius.

Gideon Haigh on Australia's 'unshakeably deadpan' – and beaten – coach; 14 September 2005.

Troy Cooley

The Tasmanian with the porn-star name.

The editor of *The Wisden Cricketer* on England's exotically named bowling coach.

Duncan Fletcher

… [an] evasively cagey hermit.

Frank Keating in the *Guardian*, 11 February 2005.

This is a fellow who makes taciturn an art form.
Mike Selvey in the *Guardian*, 7 July 2005.

Ray Jennings

It is one thing having a hard nut as a coach, quite another having simply a nut.
South African journalist Neil Manthorp on South Africa's coach Ray Jennings, quoted on cricinfo.com.

Dav Whatmore

… part national coach, part babysitter.
David Hopps on Bangladesh's coach in the *Guardian*, 10 May 2005. The average age of the Bangladesh squad for their 2005 tour of England was 22.

● THE WORLD IN DISHARMONY
the test-playing nations

A six-foot blond-haired beach bum bowling at 90mph trying to knock your head off and then telling you you're a feeble-minded tosser ... where's the problem?

Michael Atherton's view of test cricket, toned down for the official website of the Professional Cricketers' Association, before the 2001 Ashes series.

Australia

You all live in a convict colony...

An Aussie-baiting Barmy Army favourite, sung to the tune of 'Yellow Submarine'.

This is a country in which Sir Walter Raleigh would have been labelled a poofter for laying his cape over a puddle.

Martin Johnson in the *Daily Telegraph*, 27 January 2005.

On the sporting prowess of the 'convict nation':

They [the British] must have transported [to Australia] most of the athletic DNA ... along with the pickpockets and bread-snatchers.

Geoff Lawson in the *Observer*, 17 July 2005.

Pigeons and fruitflies

Australia's finest

Michael Clarke = pup (for his youth and enthusiasm)

Merv Hughes = fruitfly (for his habit of annoying his team-mates during rain delays)

Justin Langer = Mini-Tugga (for his devotion to Steve Waugh, *see below*)

Brett Lee = Bing (for a supposed resemblance to the crooner)

Glenn McGrath = pigeon (for his skinny legs, rather than his mincing run-up)

Rod Marsh = Bacchus (Bacchus Marsh is a town in Victoria)

Ricky Ponting = punter (for his enjoyment of betting)

Mark Taylor = helium bat (for his habit of lifting his bat over his shoulder and letting balls go by past the off stump)

Shane Warne = Hollywood (for his tabloid-friendly lifestyle)

Mark Waugh = Afghanistan (i.e. 'the forgotten war')

Steve Waugh = Tugga (geddit?)

Australians cannot help bragging about the inferiority of all sporting opposition because they are so racked by self-doubt … There they are … thousands of miles from the developed world, with no discernable culture or history, petrified of seeming gauche or inadequate to the grown-ups across the oceans. Sport is the only route to the global recognition they crave, so it's small surprise they do so well, or – given the chip the size of Tasmania perched on the national shoulder – that they feel the need to crow about it when they do. So remember, when next Jeff Thomson, Geoff Lawson or whoever waves his willy at poor old Blighty, that it's just a phase, and one that deserves the sympathy of a kinder elder brother.

Matthew Norman in the *Evening Standard*, 13 June 2005.

See also Ashes 2005 (pages 220–224).

Respecting the old baggy green cap

The caps were once handed out at the beginning of each tour – and, in the case of the former [Australian] captain Bill Lawry, later used to clean out his pigeon cages.
Alex Brown in the *Guardian*, 7 June 2005.

Bangladesh

Not many mothers would consider it a great idea to teach their children how to cross a road by practising on the M1 ... The only progress Bangladesh have made since being promoted five years ago is from clueless to hopeless ...

Martin Johnson on Bangladesh's grisly innings defeat by England in the first test match; in Sport.telegraph.com, 28 May 2005. Johnson warmed to his theme: 'England's batsmen plundering boundaries off Bangladesh's bowlers was the equivalent of stealing dead flies from blind spiders.'

11.30 *Today at the Test*. In the event of the Test Match finishing early, this programme will be replaced by *South Park*.

Channel 4 programme listing for highlights of the second test match between England and Bangladesh, in the *Daily Telegraph*, 6 June 2005.

A tournament that would have been more honestly labelled the Bermuda triangular.

David Hopps in the *Guardian*, 27 June 2005, as Bangladesh disappear without trace in the NatWest series.

England

I dunno. Maybe it's that tally-ho lads attitude. You know, there'll always be an England, all that Empire crap they dish out. But I never could cop Poms.
Jeff Thomson, Australian fast bowler, 1987.

All the never-say-die qualities of a kamikaze pilot.
England's cricketers in the 1990s, as seen by an Australian journalist.

English cricket is an irrelevance on and off the ground, and that's not the ramblings of an Anglophobe. It is a statement of fact.
Mike Coward, Australian cricket writer.

On England's early exit from the 1999 World Cup (held in England):
Let's get things in proportion – this was only the most catastrophic day ever for English cricket.
John Etheredge in the *Sun*, May 1999.

Is there anyone in England who can play cricket?
Headline in Sydney's *Daily Telegraph* on England's 4–1 Ashes humiliation in the 2002–2003 series in Australia.

Highlighting England's progress in the 2000s:
A few years ago England would have struggled to beat the Eskimos.
Ian Botham, quoted on cricinfo.com.

Anagrammatic England

Andrew Flintoff	=	Wendil N. Fartoff
Stephen James Harmison	=	Oh Man! Misshapen jester
Robert Key	=	OK, try beer!
Kevin Pietersen	=	Spike Intervene
Andrew Strauss	=	Dr Waster's Anus
Marcus Edward Trescothick	=	I scored a duck? Screw that, Mr!
Michael Vaughan	=	I'm Alan – huge chav
Michael P. Vaughan	=	Hum! Vaginal cheap

They have plenty of ability with no grunt, or they have plenty of grunt with no ability.

Former Australian fast bowler Merv Hughes describes the two categories into which English test cricketers can be divided; quoted in the *Guardian*, 26 April 2005.

The thing about England players is they love playing when there's no pressure on them.

Former Australian fast bowler Merv Hughes; quoted in the *Guardian*, 26 April 2005. Of England's seven wins against Australia between 1987 and 2005, six came when the Ashes were no longer at stake.

See also Ashes 2005 (pages 220–224).

New Zealand

On New Zealand's test prospects against Australia, 2004:
The reality of history suggests that [Australian prime minister] John Howard has about as much chance of becoming the Test captain as the Kiwis have of beating Australia.
Malcolm Conn; quoted on cricinfo.com.

Pakistan

Before Pakistan's inaugual tour here in 1954, the MCC secretary himself agreed to order their kit in London. On arrival, the gold-wire badge on their blazers carried the legend: PARKISTARN.
Frank Keating, 'Notes from the touchline', in the *Guardian*, 17 June 2005.

The history of Pakistani cricket is one of nepotism, inefficiency, corruption and constant bickering.
Imran Khan, quoted in Andrew John and Stephen Blake, *Cricket: it's a Funny Old Game* (2004).

South Africa

The scoreboard flashed up 'have a nice day' [when the South African-born Kevin Pietersen came in to bat], thought to be the first recorded example of South African irony.
David Hopps in the *Guardian*, 3 February 2005.

Upright, uptight underachievers.

Rob Smyth in *Spin* magazine, May 2005.

West Indies

On the 2004 series against the West Indies as England's preparation for the Ashes:

It's a bit like training for an attempt on Everest by jogging upstairs and planting a flag on the landing. The unstoppable juggernaut has been replaced by the circus clown's car – one parp on the horn and all the doors fall off.

Martin Johnson in the *Daily Telegraph*.

On Brian Lara's having the 'great misfortune to be captaining the West Indies at their lowest ebb':

Captain Ahab couldn't stop this ship from sinking.

Michael Atherton, 2004.

Zimbabwe

Most teams, you know, only the next player to bat puts pads on. With Zimbabwe, everyone puts pads on.

Zimbabwe supporter, quoted on cricinfo.com.

● ASHES 2005
The urn has turned

A sporting contest that has featured some of the loudest rows, fiercest finger-pointing and most unpleasant facial hair in the history of sport.

Harry Pearson on 130 years of Anglo-Australian rivalry; 'The Ashes 2005', in the *Guardian*, 18 July 2005.

It is currently difficult to imagine how England could face Australia over at least the next three series and have a cat in hell's chance of the Ashes.

Matthew Engel, 'Notes by the Editor', *Wisden Cricketers' Almanack* (2000).

After Australia's cricketers visited a First World War cemetery in northern France before the start of the 2005 Ashes tour:

Lighten up Aussies, it's not a war you know. Last time out it was a stop-off in Gallipoli. This year it's Normandy [sic]. What next, the salted snacks aisle in the Earls Court Tesco?

'Slogger' in the *Guardian*, 6 June 2005, suggests that the Australians might like to vary their eve-of-tour habit of visiting Australian First World War battle sites by visiting a place that bears a different Australian cultural imprint. The visit to the Australian National Memorial at Villers-Bretonneux proved a steep learning curve for the simpler souls in Ricky Ponting's squad: 'It's pretty sad and amazing how many people died in France' (all-rounder Shane Watson, 7 July).

Australia's squad [has five players] called Brad or Shane, plus there's a Brett and a Shaun. Anyone who says *Neighbours* isn't a fair dinkum reflection of Aussie life looks like a right wombat now.

'Slogger' ('A sideways glance at cricket') on the 2005 Australian Ashes squad; in the *Guardian*, 13 June 2005.

After England's 100-run defeat of Australia in their first-ever Twenty20 game:

God, it was a one-sided bore. Might as well have been playing Bangladesh.

Simon Barnes in *The Times*, 14 June 2005.

Stuffed again. Is this the worst Australian touring side ever?

Playful headline in *The Times* after Australia's defeat by Somerset, 16 June 2005.

This was royalty on the toilet, pants around their ankles.

Mike Selvey on Australia's defeat by Bangladesh in the NatWest series; in the *Guardian*, 18 June 2005.

What's worse than a whingeing Englishman? Gloating Pommies. One day we'll lose the Ashes and it will be as horrific as waking up after a night on the drink in a room full of images of Camilla Parker Bowles.

Sydney's *Daily Telegraph* hits back at the poms who have been gloating over Australia's one-day defeat by Bangladesh, June 2005.

Commenting on the rate of scoring in the 2005 Ashes test series:

Chris Tavaré, Geoff Boycott ... four runs an over? They'd have had a heart attack!

Phil Tufnell on BBC Radio Five Live, 1 September 2005.

Commenting on the age of the 2005 Australian Ashes squad:

This Australian side has more cart horses than a Victorian mail coach ... suddenly this team is looking its age. Sometimes, when the end comes, it is quick. It's been a wonderful run. Harder days lie ahead.

With the series level at 1–1, Peter Roebuck contemplates the possible end of an era; *Sydney Morning Herald*, 15 August 2005.

Just when Wimbledon was safely over, the England cricket team have set out to outdo Tim Henman as a cause of national neurosis.

Simon Barnes in *The Times*, 29 August 2005, as England took a 2–1 series lead over Australia with a nerve-jangling test victory in the fourth test match at Trent Bridge. 'Thank God there is only one more match to come,' Barnes went on, 'and we can get back to something safe such as football.'

Win or lose, we relish creating a bit of an arse-nipper.

England's Ashley Giles sums up the tension after Trent Bridge.

I'd rather lose to Bangladesh, I'd rather lose to the district women's 2nd team than lose to England.

Shannon Wilde, a resident of Shane Warne's home suburb of Black Rock, watches the fifth test match at the Oval, 12 September 2005.

Crystal balls *or just plain bollocks*

I think I was saying 3–0 or 4–0 about 12 months ago, thinking there might be a bit of rain around. But with the weather as it is at the moment, I have to say 5–0.
Glenn McGrath's prediction for the 2005 Ashes series.

England will lose the five-Test series 3–0 and the margin will be worse for them if it doesn't rain. If you put the players from Australia and England up against each other it is embarrassing. There is no contest between them on an individual or team basis.
Former Australian fast bowler Jeff Thomson, April 2005.

This England team, while they are better and on track, I can't see them beating this Australian team in a game.
Former Australian wicketkeeper Ian Healy, spring 2005.

If Australia get away to a good start then England have got no chance. They have got to be competitive in that first test at Lord's or else it's goodnight.
Former Australian seam bowler Terry Alderman. Australia won the Lord's test by 239 runs. The rest is history.

FantASHtic
URNcredible
They think it's all Oval ... it is now.
Tabloid headlines to greet England's Ashes triumph, 13 September 2005.

● SLEDGING

the not-so-subtle art of 'mental disintegration'

An inveterate absence of subtlety gave birth to sledging in the first place when New South Wales cricketer Grahame Corling made a *faux pas* at a party. It was suggested he was as 'subtle as a sledgehammer' and, while Corling went on to bask in the nickname 'Percy', after the soul singer, Australia proceeded to abuse merrrily scores of batsmen under the misnomer of 'competitive spirit'.
Rick Broadbent in *The Times*, 18 July 2005.

A sledger's dozen

Surrey batsman Smyth-Foulkes (having been bowled by Yorkshire's Emmott Robinson): Well bowled, Robinson, a wonderful delivery.
Robinson: Aye, it were bloody wasted on thee.
Exchange during a match between Surrey and Yorkshire, 1936.

Get up, I want to hit you again.
South African fast bowler Peter Heine after felling England's Peter Richardson during the 1956–7 series in South Africa; quoted in *The Wisden Cricketer*, April 2005.

As the silver-haired Northamptonshire batsman David Steele took guard against Jeff Thomson:

Who the fuck is this, Groucho Marx?

Jeff Thomson, second test match, Lord's, 1975. According to Steele, Thommo's fast bowling team-mate Dennis Lillee then snarled, 'Steeley, you little shit'; quoted by Steele himself in the *Observer Sport Monthly*, 5 June 2005.

When the young David Hookes came out to bat on his test debut:

Tony Greig: **When are your balls going to drop, sonny?**

David Hookes: **I don't know, but at least I'm playing cricket for my own country.**

Exchange during the Centenary Test Match, Melbourne 1977. Greig, the England captain, was born in South Africa.

After Barclay had been hit over the head by a bouncer from Jeff Thomson:

Barclay: **Is this a time for heroics or should we go off?**

Thomson: **I'd eff off if I were you.**

Jeff Thomson (Queensland and Australia) offers some advice to John Barclay (Eton College and Sussex), 1985.

What does your husband do when he is not watching you play cricket?

Merv Hughes to the hapless Graeme Hick, who had endured a barrage of bouncers from the Australian.

After Merv Hughes had launched a barrage of bouncers at Hick, punctuated by sledges:

Umpire 'Dickie' Bird: Mervyn, Mervyn, what has poor Mr Hick ever done to you?

Merv Hughes: He offended me in a former life.

Quoted in the *Guardian*, 26 April 2005.

Hi mate, I've waited two years for this and I'm going to send you right back to the fucking shrink.

Shane Warne torments South African batsman Daryll Cullinan; quoted by Piers Morgan in the *Observer Sport Monthly*, 5 June 2005. Cricket folklore has it that when Cullinan confessed to seeing a psychiatrist after a torrid run of performances against Warne, the spinner greeted his return to the crease with the above words.

Queensland captain: I want a fielder right under [Nasser] Hussain's nose.

Ian Healy: That could mean anywhere within three miles.

Exchange recalled by Hussain himself, quoted in *Spin* magazine, May 2005.

Umpires and umpiring

I would rather spend eight hours a day undergoing root-canal treatment than function as an international umpire.
Matthew Engel, 'Notes by the Editor', *Wisden Cricketers' Almanack* 2005.

Response to a batsman's complaint at not being able to see the ball during a late-finishing Gillette Cup match in the 1970s:
You can see the moon, son, how far do you want to see?
Anon. umpire; quoted by Martin Johnson in the *Daily Telegraph*, 13 June 2005.

After Bird had turned down a vociferous lbw appeal:
Dennis Lillee: I think your eyesight's going, Dickie.
Dickie Bird: No, it's your eyesight that's going. I'm the ice-cream seller.
Quoted in *A Century of Cricket Jokes* (1996).

Describing West Indian umpire Steve Bucknor, notorious for his slow decision-making:
A lingering death merchant.
Herny Blofeld.

Describing the ample-girthed David Shepherd:
... a much-loved avuncular pudding wrapped in an umpire's coat ...
Tanya Aldred in the *Guardian*, 18 April 2005. Shepherd once ended a test match session with the words: 'It's tea, and that means scones and Devonshire clotted cream.'

Put a Mars Bar on a good length. That should do it.

Australian wicketkeeper Ian Healy to Shane Warne, who had been trying to tempt the portly Sri Lankan batsman Arjuna Ranatunga to jump out of his crease and drive.

Mark Waugh: Fuck me, look who it is. Mate, what are you doing out here? There's no way you're good enough to play for England.
James Ormond: Maybe not, but at least I'm the best player in my family.

Exchange between Waugh and the England seamer when Ormond came out to bat during the 2001 Ashes series.

Watermelons.

The name with which Shane Warne and his Hampshire team-mates sledged the Sussex wicketkeeper Matt Prior, on account of his well-developed pectoral musculature, during Hampshire's County Championship match with Sussex at Hove, April 2005. Warne's sledging of Prior led to public criticism of Warne by Sussex captain Chris Adams, to which Warne replied that he was merely responding to Matt Prior's 'chesting' of Hampshire's Simon Katich. 'I thought cricket was a non-contact sport,' Warne wrote in his *Times* column. 'I was sticking up for my mate and letting Prior know what I thought about his behaviour.' According to Derek Pringle, writing in the *Daily Telegraph*, Warne's use of the 'Watermelons' nickname 'caused so much hilarity that Simon Katich, another member of the Australian touring party, was temporarily unable to bowl'.

Whoooooooohh!!!

Darren Gough treats Australia's Shane Watson to a ghost impression during England's second NatWest trophy game, June 2005. Watson had been so spooked by tales of ghosts in Durham's Lumley Castle, where the Australian team were staying, that he slept on team-mate Brett Lee's floor ('the stuff with Watto was blown a bit out of proportion, but it was true that he slept on the floor of my room'). Australia's media officer Belinda Dennett said: 'I saw ghosts. I swear I'm telling the truth. I looked out of the window and saw a procession of white people walking past. It was very scary.' The *Observer*'s Kevin Mitchell described Gough's action as 'the best mimed sledge seen on an English cricket field in living memory' (26 June); after what one journalist described as 'Nightmare on Chester-le-Street', Watson looked odds-on to be greeted by choruses of the *Ghostbusters* theme for the rest of the Ashes summer. *See also* Shane Watson (page 205).

● THE COMMENTARY BOX
lounge lizards and prep school masters

Test Match Special, like the MCC, Lord's and the late, ghastly E.W. Swanton, represents the 'jolly good chap' view of cricket, one that squeals with delight over a batsman's public school pedigree and still takes a dim view of wearing shades on the field.
Leo McKinstry in the *Observer Sport Monthly*, February 2005.

Jonathan Agnew

… like some pompous prep school master.
Leo McKinstry in the *Observer Sport Monthly*, February 2005, on Aggers's calling for the then England captain Mike Atherton to resign over the dirt-in-the-pocket episode in 1994.

Henry Blofeld

Take those marbles out of your mouth.
Former Australian batsman Jack Fingleton to Blofeld.

Michael Holding

His Jamaican tones are deeper than the collected works of Jean-Paul Sartre.
The Wisden Cricketer on the West Indies paceman-turned-Sky Sports commentator, June 2005.

John Howard

A serial infiltrator of the commentary box ... there are blind wombats with a better feel for what's happening on the field.
Marina Hyde reacts to the news that the Australian prime minister will be attending the Lord's test match; the *Guardian*, 18 July 2005.

Mark Nicholas

If he can't learn the importance of modesty and silence from the immortal Richie Benaud, he should bugger off and try his luck as an ersatz Philip Schofield.
Matthew Norman on Mark Nicholas, *Evening Standard*, 24 May 2004.

Smoother than Henry Blofeld's smoking-jacket.
The *Wisden Cricketer* on Channel 4's cricket anchorman, 'All miked up and ready to go', June 2005.

Commentary classics

On the outfield, hundreds of small boys are playing with their balls.
Rex Alston.

Patel took it down on his knees in front of slip.
Jonathan Agnew.

After Mike Atherton was struck in the box by a delivery that lifted sharply off a length:

David Gower: Well, Richie, that ball certainly bounced.

Richie Benaud: Yeeees, David. [pause] But which one?

Anecdote told by Matthew Norman in the *Evening Standard*, 13 June 2005.

He's usually a good puller, but he couldn't get it up that time.
Richie Benaud.

What a magnificent shot! No! He's out!
Tony Greig.

And a sedentary seagull flies by.
Brian Johnston, quoted in Andrew John and Stephen Blake, *Cricket: it's a Funny Old Game* (2004).

Play Mark Nicholas bingo!

Juuuust exquisite!

Glenn McGrath!

Remarkable man, remarkable cricketer!

Gee!

Oh yes. Oh yes, yes, yes!

To die for!

Goodness gracious!

Oh my…!

Crackerjack off-drive!

Spin magazine invites readers to 'tick off the phrases as you hear them', August 2005.

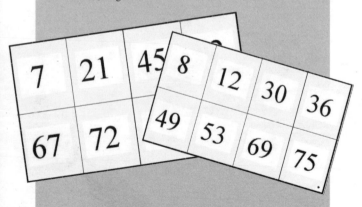

Could Mark Nicholas be the next Bond villain?
'Terrace top ten' in *Spin* magazine, July 2005.

Dermot Reeve

N is for ... Nipple Ring, as worn by Dermot Reeve.
Strange but true. Marcus Berkmann, the A to Z of 2004, in
The Wisden Cricketer, January 2005.

Posh in a lounge lizard sort of way.
The Wisden Cricketer analyses Reeve's accent, June 2005.

Bob Willis

So dull is he, tapes of the Willis delivery should be sold in Mothercare as a sleeping aid for fractious toddlers.
Jim White on Bob Willis as a Sky TV commentator.

Bob Willis ... may well be the unnamed broadcaster described ... in a recent book ... as sounding as if he'd just attended the cremation of his pet dog.
Philip Derriman in the *Sydney Morning Herald*, 25 June 2005.

RUGBY UNION

Cauliflower ears and arse-slapping

A sport where players have their faces torn open, sewn back together without anaesthetic and then run back on the pitch.

Annabel Rivkin, 'This sporting life', in *ES* magazine, 28 January 2005.

A ridiculous sport.

Phil Vickery, quoted by Robert Kitson in the *Guardian*, 12 February 2005.

League or Union?

League is much, much more physical than Union, and that's before anyone starts breaking the rules.

Adrian Hadley, 1988.

It's the first time I've been cold for seven years. I was never cold playing rugby league.

Jonathan Davis on returning to rugby union; on *A Question of Sport*, BBC TV, 1995.

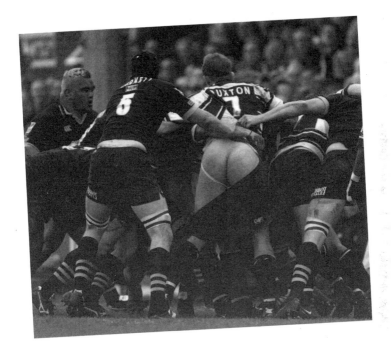

It's the only sport I know where
you can put your head up the
other player's bum and the referee
allows it.

Ally McCoist on *A Question of Sport*.

● THE PLAYERS
Lewd gorillas and stroppy frogs

The line of cauliflower ears resembles a Bow Street identity parade in Victorian times for a round-up of Magwitches bound for a convict hulk and the colonies.
Frank Keating watches the singing of the national anthems; in the *Guardian*, 4 February 2005.

… there is a fine line between being a great rugby player and a thug.
Ken Laban, friend and coach of Tana Umaga (*see* page 251); quoted by James Lawton in the *Independent*, 30 June 2005.

The sidestep is the small man's act of retribution. In a game of big men this is one moment of revenge.
Former Welsh winger Gerald Davies; quoted in the *Guardian*, 21 March 2005.

Neil Back

… knee-high to a grasshopper by modern standards …
Chris Hewett in the *Independent*, 13 June 2005.

When asked if he regretted shoving referee Steve Lander after
Leicester's cup final defeat by Bath at Twickenham, May 1996:

I regret not taking a 30-metre run-up.
Back himself, quoted by Robert Kitson in the *Guardian*, 7 June 2005.

Philippe Bernat-Salles

A stroppy little Frog.
Steve Smith on the silver-haired French winger of the 1990s; BBC TV
commentary on Five Nations rugby, mid-1990s.

Will Carling

I'd rather crawl across broken glass naked than
speak to Will Carling.
Dick Best, quoted in the *Daily Mail*, 28 April 2005. Harlequins fired
Best as their coach in May 1997 following a dressing-room revolt led
by… Will Carling.

Colin Charvis

At least this time I haven't been the subject of a
poll comparing me with Saddam Hussein and
Osama bin Laden.
Colin Charvis, the captain of Wales, speaking about his popularity in
the Principality; quoted in *The Times*, quotes of the year, 2004.

Lawrence Dallaglio

Talking about life after rugby union:

If I haven't taken too many bangs on the head by the end of my career, I might just start thinking about using my brain again.

Lawrence Dallaglio.

A lewd, clean gorilla.

Anagram of Lawrence Dallaglio's name.

Matt Dawson

Anne Robinson: Matt, why do you think they are getting rid of you? You haven't answered a question incorrectly.

Matt Dawson: It's their loss – their loss.

Anne Robinson: It's not that you're a little bit arrogant is it, Matt?

From the special rugby edition of *The Weakest Link*, BBCTV; quoted in the *Evening Standard*, 2 February 2005.

Harry Ellis

England's 'dirty' Harry.

Punning headline to an article in the *Evening Standard*, 10 February 2005.

Andy Farrell

Following Farrell's move from rugby league to rugby union:

The man is just another journeyman plodder.
Honest and brave – but cart-horse slow.

Derek 'Robbo' Robson, The Tees Mouth, on bbc.co.uk, May 2005.

Danny Grewcock

A fuse desperately seeking a match.

Robert Kitson on England's combustible lock forward; in the
Guardian, 7 February 2005.

A one-man oil refinery.

Chris Hewett in the *Independent*, 13 June 2005.

Gavin Henson

… since when did a Welsh centre three-quarter
wear a fake tan, spiked hair and silver boots? Did
the legendary Bleddyn Williams take the field in
full make-up? I don't think so.

William Donaldson and Hermione Eyre, *The Dictionary of National
Celebrity* (2005).

The David Beckham of Welsh rugby.

Oh dear. Phil Bennett, quoted in the *Evening Standard*, 4 February
2005.

Groomin' awful   Henson's hair

... his hair could give a small dog a run for its money. It stands, dyed red and glossy, bolt upright at least two inches high. He gets through tins of Dax Wave and Groom at the rate old-fashioned rugby players sank beer. Tanya Aldred in the *Guardian*, 4 June 2005.

Gavin and Charlotte

texting Taffs

Singer Charlotte Church was said to be 'very embarrassed' after a topless picture she texted to her boyfriend was passed on to hundreds of other mobile phone users. The 19-year-old sent the photograph to Welsh rugby star Gavin Henson in a series of texts between the couple.

'Exposed: Charlotte's topless text', *Evening Standard*, 30 March 2005.

[Gavin and Charlotte] may just have the potential to make David and Posh look like characters from *Brideshead Revisited*.

James Lawton in the *Independent*, 28 June 2005.

[In his guest appearance on *Hell's Kitchen*] Henson … was startled by the revelation that the turbot was a fish rather than a souped-up car.

Donald McRae in the *Guardian*, 9 May 2005.

His shyness is derivative of not having a high intellect.

Former Welsh centre and Swansea captain Scott Gibbs, quoted by Tanya Aldred in the *Guardian*, 4 June 2005. Gibbs added: 'If I'd turned up with fake tan and hairless, Peter Winterbottom and Mike Teague would have thrown me out of the hotel.'

Gavin Henson, the conceited Welsh centre three-quarter, will be hit as if by a wrecking-ball from outer space, his various parts being redistributed around the field, once Mike Tindall is fit enough to resume his duties in England's three-quarter line.
William Donaldson and Hermione Eyre.

Describing Henson's reaction to being left out of the Lions squad for the first test match against New Zealand, 2005:
A one-man *eisteddfod* of bruised sensibilities.
James Lawton in the *Independent*, 28 June 2005. 'Some claim that Henson now has the unofficial world record for slamming doors without quite detaching them from their hinges.'

Announcing that Henson was not suffering from concussion:
Gavin's mental faculties are as intact as they were when he came on the tour. We can do some things in medical science but we can't do others.
Lions' doctor James Robson; quoted in the *Guardian*, 7 July 2005.

The most exotic thing to come out of Neath.
Michael Aylwin in the *Observer*, 30 January 2005.

Charlie Hodgson

You can't kick.

Australian sledge to Hodgson during England's game with Australia, 27 November 2004. After Australia's 21–19 victory, courtesy of a Hodgson penalty miss, the Sale No.10 admitted that the Australians had 'got to him'.

Once and for all, I'm not a second Jonny Wilkinson.

Hodgson before England v. France at Twickenham, 12 February 2005. To prove the point he proceeded to fluff a straightforward drop goal that would have given England victory in the game's dying minutes. One journalist remarked: 'Alas, poor Hodgson!'.

Adam Jones

A giant furball.

BBC TV commentary during Wales's 2005 Six Nations match against Scotland, describing the curly-maned Welsh forward.

Josh Lewsey

Little Lord Fauntleroy's head on the Terminator's body.

Anon. rugby journalist, c.2004.

… imagine a cherub after 12 rounds with Joe Frazier.
Chris Hewett on Lewsey's 'beaten-up face' after New Zealand's 48–18 victory over the Lions in the second test match; in the *Independent*, 4 July 2005.

Martin Johnson

A Mount Rushmore of a face.
Gerald Davies on the craggy Johnson; in *The Times*, 28 January 2005.

Reflecting on his rugby career as his retirement approached:
Deep down I am still the same old miserable man.
Quoted in the *Evening Standard*, 12 May 2005.

The lad who put the 'rough' into Market Harborough.
Hugh Godwin in the *Independent on Sunday*, 16 May 2005.

The fellow with the demeanour of Burke and Hare.
Hugh Godwin.

Frédéric Michalak

One of the flakiest No 10s in the world.
William Fotheringham in the *Guardian*, 22 March 2005.

Michalak … has been down the catwalk for Christian Lacroix, has posed naked for the fashion magazine *Citizen K* and has been proclaimed – to his great consternation – a gay icon by a French gossip magazine.

William Fotheringham.

Lewis Moody

England's most buoyant arse-slapper.

Donald McRae in the *Guardian*, 21 February 2005.

The mad freak.

Steve Thompson's name for his gung-ho team-mate; quoted by Chris Jones in the *Evening Standard*, 30 June 2005.

Graham Rowntree

Rowntree's ears are a stark warning of the aesthetic dangers of prolonged exposure to the rugby scrum … they resemble those indeterminate, gristly things given to puppies to chew on.

Derek Potter, *Down Among the Head Men* (2002).

Matthew Tait

An 18-year-old wonder until Saturday and a 19-year-old reject today.

Nigel Melville as 'rugby's fresh-faced angel of the north' is dropped for England's Six Nations game against France; in the *Guardian*, 10 February 2005. Tait celebrated his birthday the day after making his début in England's 11–9 defeat by Wales, the world champions' seventh defeat in ten matches.

Gareth Thomas

On being asked whether Thomas would ever make a captain:

The short answer's no, and the long answer's no as well.

Former Welsh coach Graham Henry, quoted in the *Guardian*, 29 June 2005. Thomas led Wales to the 2005 Six Nations grand slam and replaced Brian O'Driscoll as Lions captain after the latter dropped out of the 2005 Lions tour of New Zealand through injury.

Steve Thompson

On the England's hooker's line-out throwing:

More Eric Sykes than Eric Bristow.

Chris Hewett in the *Independent*, 11 February 2005. 'Andy Robinson, the head coach, described the big Midlander's inaccuracies as "disappointing" – Robbo-speak for "diabolical".'

Mike Tindall

Too much horse riding.

Jibe directed, since 2004, at the injured Tindall. In 2003 the England World Cup star began a relationship with the eventing royal Zara Phillips, daughter of Princess Anne and Captain Mark Phillips.

Tana Umaga

Wanted for the assassination of Brian O'Driscoll, June 25th 2005.

T-shirt slogan accompanying a photograph of Tana Umaga sported by a Lions fan after Umaga's and Keven Mealamu's notorious 'spear tackle' of the Lions captain during the first Lions v. New Zealand test match, which ended O'Driscoll's tour (*see* page 261). Another t-shirt slogan was: 'Keven Mealamu, Tana Umaga and Michael Jackson are innocent. Yeh, right.'

Physically, competitively, Tana is a beast ... If you finish up in the hospital he might send you flowers, but he won't worry about you. To be honest, after the O'Driscoll incident he was probably thinking, 'Who's next, Gavin Henson?'

Umaga's friend and coach Ken Laban; quoted by James Lawton in the *Independent*, 30 June 2005.

... a man of such ferocious aspect that he makes Cerberus the three-headed hound of Hades look like Miffy.

Harry Pearson in the *Guardian*, 9 July 2005.

Phil Vickery

Raging Bull looks more like Raging Stag these days.

Robert Kitson, 'Vickery is back leaner but wiser', in the *Guardian*, 12 February 2005.

Shouted to Vickery after he was involved in a dust-up with a Worcester player at Kingsholm:

Oi, Vicks – I hit my wife harder than that.

Gloucester fan; quoted by Robert Kitson in the *Guardian*, 12 February 2005.

Jonny Wilkinson

The perennial English patient.

Robert Kitson puns on Michael Ondaatje's Booker Prize-winning novel to sum up a year of injury misery that ruled Wilkinson out of the 2005 Six Nations; in the *Guardian*, 15 March 2005.

He has now featured in more hospital dramas in the past 15 months than the cast of *Casualty*, *Green Wing* and *Holby City* combined.

Robert Kitson.

If his failing fitness proves he cannot hack it, there is always Hackett.

Robert Kitson.

Why does Hackett dress him up as if he were an effeminate fop on the lines of *Brideshead Revisited*?

Peter Oborne in the *Evening Standard*, 9 May 2005.

J.P.R. Williams

Reacting to Williams being involved in a road accident:

Bloody typical, isn't it? The car's a write-off. The tanker's a write-off. But JPR comes out of it all in one piece.

Gareth Edwards, 1978.

Shane Williams

Comparing hairstyles sported in the France v. Wales match in the 2005 Six Nations:

Aurélien Rougerie sported the flowing locks of a Renaissance courtier; Shane Williams the blond streaks normally associated with shopping-mall chavs.

Anon. rugby journalist.

... bouncing off collisions like a dodgem car made by Matchbox.

Chris Hewett explains why Shane Williams's attempts at tackling 'will be slaughtered' by journalists after his performance in the second Lions test match v. New Zealand; in the *Independent*, 4 July 2005.

Joe Worsley

On his 'trout pout' look after being punched in the mouth by Neil Back in the Wasps v. Leicester Zurich premiership grand final, 14 May 2005:

I look a bit like Lesley Ash after the collagen implant.

Worsley himself.

Kevin Yates

A player of ours has been proven guilty of biting – that's a scar that will never heal.

Bath coach Andy Robinson after his prop forward Kevin Yates was suspended for taking a chunk out of an opposing flanker's ear.

● THE COACHES
hungry crocodiles and mad professors

Graham Henry

Tuesday 12 June 2001: Beat Queensland President's XV 83–6. Just before boarding bus for ground, get pep talk from GH. Bit over the top ... crap function afterwards.

Thursday 14 June: More mindless training. Coaching staff taking it too far ...

Tuesday 19 June: Lost to Australia A 28–25. GH does pre-match but doesn't inspire me at all. Too much screaming and shouting.

From Matt Dawson's newspaper diary of the 2001 Lions tour of Australia, when the Lions were coached by New Zealander Henry.

One is ... reminded of Roald Dahl's hungry crocodile, pretending to be a park bench in order to get closer to his prospective human lunch.

Robert Kitson on New Zealand's wily coach at the start of the 2005 Lions tour; in the *Guardian*, 7 June 2005.

Bernard Laporte

... for mad-professor capriciousness, none of those three supremos [Sven-Göran Eriksson, Duncan Fletcher and Andy Robinson] can remotely match France's rugby coach Bernard Laporte, whose creative fantasies in selection and conception match only his own physical resemblance to a hare-brained and wild-eyed Hollywood sci-fi boffin.

Frank Keating, 'Notes from the touchline', in the *Guardian*, 11 February 2005.

Andy Robinson

The reticently irresolute, muffle-toned Andy Robinson.

Frank Keating in the *Guardian*, 11 February 2005.

Andy Robinson's level of failure as new England rugby coach is little short of spectacular.

Matthew Norman in the *Evening Standard*, 14 February 2005.

Clive Woodward

Sir Wacky Woodward.
Frank Keating in the *Guardian*, 4 February 2005.

I'm not a homosexual but I realize now that I loved Clive Woodward.
Bernard Laporte, quoted in *The Sunday Times*, 13 February 2005.

I am beginning to wonder if Clive Woodward knows what he is doing.
Welsh legend J.P.R. Williams is dismayed by the axing of Welsh internationals Gavin Henson, Michael Owen and Martin Williams from the Lions' side to face New Zealand in the first test match; quoted in the *Evening Standard*, 20 June 2005.

Wrong numbers, Clive

26–5
The try count against Woodward in his last six test matches as an international rugby coach.

0800 won-nothing, won-nothing, won-nothing.
The freephone helpline number suggested to Woodward by New Zealanders for him to pour out his problems after the Lions' 3–0 test drubbing by the All Blacks, June–July 2005.

Woodward for director of football? May the Saints preserve him...

Martin Samuel on Woodward's new role at recently relegated Southampton football club; headline in *The Times*, 23 June 2005.

Describing the effect on Woodward's reputation of the Lions' 21–3 defeat by the All Blacks in the first test match:

Before breakfast on Saturday, Woodward was rugby union's Sir Alf Ramsey and in less time than it takes cold egg to congeal on a greasy plate he became its Graham Taylor.

Martin Samuel, 'Time's nearly up, Turnip!' in *The Times*, 29 June 2005.

Slightly delusional.

For maximum effect, say it in a Welsh accent. Charlotte Church on the Lions coach, who left her boyfriend Gavin Henson out of the Lions' XV for the first test against the All Blacks; quoted in *The Times*, 30 June 2005 (*see also* Gavin Henson, page 243).

Sir Clive Woodward was knighted for services to rugby but I'd say they should look at revoking it when he gets home.

Former All Black prop Richard Loe, July 2005.

… **unhealthily in thrall to his own genius.**
Richard Williams on Woodward following the Lions' 3–0 defeat by
the All Blacks, July 2005, in the *Guardian*, 11 July 2005.

Is Sir Clive a psychopath?
New Zealand Herald, July 2005.

As Woodward began a two-week, post-Lions tour fishing holiday
before starting a career in football with Southampton:
I think the fish can rest easy.
Anon. journalist, quoted on scrum.com.

See also 'Lost in the Land of the Long White Cloud' (pages 260–261).

Lost in the Land of the Long White Cloud

Lions are lousy lovers.

Headline in a New Zealand newspaper during the 1977 Lions tour of New Zealand spawned by the exploits of 'Wanda from Wanganui', who claimed to have slept with four of the touring side, but was disppointed by the experience. 'I found them boring, self-centred, ruthless, always on the make and anything but exciting bedmates.'

Brian O'Driscoll's pride of pussycats.

New Zealand *Sunday News*, 12 June 2005, following the Lions' 19–13 defeat by the New Zealand Maori.

The 2005 Lions are mince and potatoes billed as exotic fare.

Gregor Paul in the New Zealand *Herald on Sunday*, 12 June 2005.

Describing the Lions team that faced New Zealand in the first test match:

England plus-a-few-Celts.

Paul Hayward in the *Daily Telegraph*, 25 June 2005.

Nice PR: shame about the rugby.

Guardian headline, 27 June 2005, following the Lions' 21–3 first test defeat by New Zealand. The allusion is to the way Sir Clive Woodward's PR team, led by Alastair Campbell, handled the incident in which Brian O'Driscoll dislocated his shoulder (*see below*).

A steaming heap of horrors.

Robert Kitson on the Lions' 21–3 first test defeat by New Zealand; in the *Guardian*, 27 June 2005.

Spear and Loathing.

How one wit described the events of the first Lions v. New Zealand test match, 25 June 2005, in which a controversial 'spear tackle' (the tacklers grab a leg apiece and dump the tackled player on his head) by All Blacks captain Tana Umaga and hooker Keven Mealamu left Lions captain Brian O'Driscoll with a dislocated shoulder and out of the tour just 40 seconds into the game (*see also* Tana Umaga, page 251).

If you were horses you'd have been shot.

Al Murray, the 'pub landlord', spots wounded Lions Richard Hill and Tom Shanklin in the audience for his stand-up act in Wellington, July 2005.

The trouble with these Lions is that they don't sleep together.

Former (1971) Lion J.P.R. Williams diagnoses the malaise affecting the 2005 Lions after a 48–18 mauling by the All Blacks in the Wellington 'Caketin' gave New Zealand an unassailable 2–0 series lead: 'They don't room together, they don't get to know each other. They all have single rooms and retreat into themselves'; quoted in the *Daily Telegraph*, 4 July 2005.

● INTERNATIONAL RUGBY

England

Most Misleading Campaign of 1991: England's rugby World Cup squad, who promoted a scheme called 'Run with the Ball'. Not, unfortunately, among themselves.
Time Out, 1991.

I didn't know Father Christmas was English.
Thomas Castaignède after England's 18–17 Six Nations defeat by France at Twickenham, 13 February 2005. Robert Kitson commented in the *Guardian* (14 February): 'To be beaten by France is one thing; to go down to possibly the least ambitious French team of all time having led 17–6 at half-time is quite another kettle of poisson.'

We were not fairly beaten, My Lord. No Englishman is ever fairly beaten.
George Bernard Shaw, *St Joan*, Act IV. A possible epitaph for England's 19–13 defeat by Ireland in Dublin, 27 February 2005, in which England coach Andy Robinson felt that, amongst other refereeing errors, England had been denied two good tries.

See also pages 264–265.

France

Describing the French team that somehow managed to defeat
England at Twickenham, February 2005:

Displaying the cutting edge of an elderly poodle.

Robert Kitson in the *Guardian*, 14 February 2005. *See also* page 264.

The best of Murray Mexted

Sublime handling skills, childish double-entendres

There's nothing that a tight forward likes more than a
loosie right up his backside.

I don't like this new law, because your first instinct when
you see a man on the ground is to go down on him.

He's looking for some meaningful penetration into the
backline.

I can tell you it's a magnificent feeling when the gap
opens up and you burst right through.

You don't like to see hookers going down on players
like that.

Everybody knows that I have been pumping Martin
Leslie for a couple of seasons now.

Murray Mexted, former All Black, now a colourful TV
commentator.

Champs to chumps

England's *annus horribilis*, 2004–5

Sportspeople say you don't become a bad side overnight. The England rugby side provide a spectacular refutation of that supposedly immutable law … I can tell you the night over which England became bad … November 22, 2003. England won the World Cup that night: and by dawn the world had fallen apart.

Simon Barnes in *The Times*, 14 February 2005.

About as threatening as the Black Knight in *Monty Python and the Holy Grail*, famous for his stubborn belief in his own invincibility despite an increasing lack of limbs.

Robert Kitson on England in the 2005 Six Nations; in the *Guardian*, 7 February 2005.

A contest between two old men in a brothel, fighting over the last Viagra tablet.
Richard Williams on France's Six Nations victory over England at Twickenham; in the *Guardian*, 14 February 2005.

An Englishman cryogenically frozen on the night of England's World Cup victory on 22 November 2003 and brought back to life on the evening of 19 March 2005 would struggle to comprehend the nightmare that has engulfed English rugby: fourth in the Six Nations table? Wales grand slam champions? Gavin Henson – a man who waxes his leg hair and goes out with Charlotte Church – acclaimed by serious rugby journalists as a world-class centre? It can't be true, it can't.
Anon. English rugby fan following Wales's grand slam-clinching victory over Ireland, 19 March 2005; 'Land of My Barbers', on ventyourEnglishspleen.com.

Take that, Anne Robinson. I am sure her face fell when she heard the glad tidings from Cardiff or would have done had surgical procedures not now made that a physical impossibility.
Martin Kelner in the *Guardian* following Wales's capture of the 2005 grand slam; 21 March 2005.

Ireland

Traditionally Irish sides react about as positively to the tag of favourites as a highly strung stallion does to first-time blinkers.
Robert Kitson in the *Guardian*, 27 January 2005.

You have to view the Irish as perpetual chokers.
Former Lions and England coach Dick Best following Ireland's loss to France, which destroyed their hopes of a grand slam; quoted in the *Evening Standard*, 15 March 2005.

The Portugal of rugby union.
Richard Williams deplores 'the failure of Ireland's gifted generation to bear the promised fruit'; in the *Guardian*, 22 March 2005.

New Zealand

Remember that rugby is a team game: all 14 of you make sure you pass the ball to Jonah.
Anonymous fax message to the All Blacks before the 1995 World Cup semi-final against England. They passed to Jonah, and the rest is history.

We are not calling them the All Blacks this week. They are New Zealand, which is just a poxy little island in the Pacific Ocean.
Scott Johnson, the assistant Wales coach and an Australian, gives his verdict on his Antipodean neighbours. Johnson later remarked: 'I apologise to all New Zealanders. In fact, it's two islands'; quoted in

The Times, quotes of the year, 2004. When Johnson arrived at Auckland airport in June 2005, he was briefly kept waiting by a huge immigration official who examined his passport in minute detail before remarking: 'A thousand welcomes to our poxy little island in the Pacific. I do hope your stay with us isn't too awful' (quoted in the *Daily Telegraph*, 24 June 2005).

Fear and loathing across the Tasman Sea

During a Wallaby tour of New Zealand some years ago, one of the Australian players had an affair with a local girl in Wellington. The team moved on, the girl stayed behind, and the whole thing was forgotten about.

Four years later, however, the same player returns to New Zealand with another Wallaby touring side. The team is in Wellington, when who should he see but his former lover with a small child. He runs up to her and greets her, and asks if the child is his. 'Yes,' she says, 'it is.' 'But why didn't you tell me?' he asks. 'Well,' she replies, 'after I found out I was pregnant, I invited all the members of my family together to discuss the matter – my grandparents, my parents, my uncles, aunts and cousins. And we all came to the same conclusion: we would rather the child was a bastard than have an Australian for a father.'

Scotland

Even Bill McLaren might have been temped to switch channels.

Ian Malin on Scotland's Six Nations game with Italy ('a game in monochrome … full of mistakes and devoid of imagination'), 26 February 2005; in the *Guardian*, 28 February 2005.

Wales

Morbid footballism.

North Walian former Liberal prime minister David Lloyd George on the South Walian passion for rugby, quoted in the *Independent*, 8 February 2005.

Bad hair Dai!

A victory not for running rugby but for chav hairstyles of the worst conceivable kind: Dwane Peel's bogbrush, the preening Henson's gelled spikes, and – chief offender in a catalogue of gents' hairdressing awfulness – Shane Williams's streaked mullet.

Anon. English rugby fan following Wales's grand slam-clinching victory over Ireland, 19 March 2005; 'Land of My Barbers', on ventyourEnglishspleen.com.

It's almost as if they have had a makeover from Trinny and Susannah.

Nick Mullins, BBC TV commentator, on Wales's second-half renaissance that brought victory in their Six Nations match against France, 26 February 2005.

Could we base the Lions test team on Wales? Absolutely not … their whole game plan is built on sand.

Former Lions and England coach Dick Best, quoted in 'Don't select too many Welshmen', in the *Evening Standard*, 15 March 2005. Best advises Lions coach Sir Clive Woodward against picking too many Welsh players for the Lions tour of New Zealand following a 'quirky Six Nations' in which France and England's 'disarray' has allowed Wales to 'come through'. *See also* Lost in the Land of the Long White Cloud (pages 260–261).

TENNIS

Wham, Bam, thank you ma'am

A depressingly petit bourgeois game.
Matthew Norman in the *Evening Standard*, 31 January 2005.

… tennis is a pleasant pastime for foreign girls and and the more delicate sort of boy and it is for this reason that I regard England's long-term failure to produce a men's singles champion as a badge of national honour … the average Englishwomen is likewise far too robust to be bothering with a pastime as unashamedly cardigan-friendly as tennis.
Harry Pearson in the *Guardian*, 25 June 2005.

Describing modern tennis, dominated by power hitting:
It's all, as David Bowie said, 'Wham, bam, thank you ma'am.'
John McEnroe, quoted by Tim Adams in *Being John McEnroe* (2004).

Tennis is the only sport that requires its spectators to be quieter than the players.
Jeremy Davis ponders a very noisy Wimbledon, July 2005 (*see* pages 293–294).

● THE PLAYERS
pantalones and camel noises

André Agassi

More Rod Stewart than Rod Laver.
Robert Philip in the *Daily Telegraph*, 28 January 2005.

Sue Barker

… Sue Barker is to the womanhood of Albion what the Pekinese is to the world of dogs – all very well if you want something cute to carry around in a shoulder bag, but useless at scaring away burglars or herding frisky bullocks.
Harry Pearson in the *Guardian*, 25 June 2005.

Boris Becker

… with his wild staring eyes and vertical white hair, [he looks] for all the world like a cartoon character who has just bumped into a headless phantom.
Harry Pearson in the *Guardian*, 25 June 2005.

'Strenuous singles we played after tea...'

British tennis

... when English people say they can play tennis they don't mean what Americans mean when they say they can play tennis.

The character of John Self in Martin Amis's novel *Money* (1984).

On the British obsession with Wimbledon:

For the English, tennis is not so much a sport as a fortnight.

Tim Adams in *Being John McEnroe* (2004). 'For two weeks a year you would have the impression that tennis was a vivid national obsession ... then, for the remaining fifty weeks of the year, save when Britain is losing a zonal Davis Cup match to Paraguay or Turkey: nothing.'

Here's a little factoid for all those who delight in belittling British tennis: the small holiday island of Majorca has twice as many players in the world's top ten as we have.

Jon Henderson in the *Observer*, 8 May 2005. The players in question were Carlos Moya (No. 8) and teenage sensation Rafael ('Rafa') Nadal (No. 7). The Briton was, of course, 'Tiger Tim' Henman, but he would be out of the top ten by the end of Wimbledon 2005.

On the middle-class-ness of British tennis players:

Every one of them ... emitted the gentle aroma of the freshly mown rectory lawn.

Matthew Norman in the *Evening* Standard, 27 June 2005. 'Virginia Wade, Sue Barker, Annabel Croft, Jo Durie, Roger Taylor, Mark Cox, Buster Mottram, John Lloyd, and, par excellence, Tim Henman ... until now [i.e. the emergence of Andrew Murray] every highly ranked British tennis player ... has been, or seemed to be, luminescently middle class.'

Castle ... was once Britain's No. 1 tennis player ... during an era ... when we were not very strong in the sport (Tommy Cooper, I think, was No. 4 at the time).

Martin Kelner on Andrew Castle in the *Guardian*, 27 June 2005.

Sergi Bruguera

... a graduate of the Spanish Inquisition school of tennis.

Robert Philip on the 'remarkably mind-numbing Sergi Bruguera' (two times winner of the French Open, 1993–4); in the *Daily Telegraph*, 24 May 2005.

Kim Clijsters

La laitière flamande ('The Flemish milkmaid').

Anon. French journalist on the prosaic Belgian, 2005.

Jill Craybas

... a 31-year-old of such obscurity that I doubt even her mother's ever heard of her ... Jill Craybas sounds like a Cajun seafood, and usually plays like one.

Matthew Norman in the *Evening* Standard, 27 June 2005, on the shadowy American conqueror of Serena Williams (*see* page 296) in the third round of Wimbledon 2005.

Lindsay Davenport

... Davenport has the turning circle of a station wagon ...

Mike Dickson on the losing finalist at Wimbledon 2005; in the *Daily Mail*, 28 June 2005.

Kim and Lleyton — why?

The fact that she has reached four grand slam finals without winning one of them raises some pretty big questions about [Kim] Clijsters – none of them half as big, however, as what possessed her to go out with Lleyton Hewitt.

Jeremy Davis, July 2005.

Explaining the exclusion of Clijsters and Hewitt from a selection of the 'top ten sporting love matches':

… neither good nor good-looking enough to make the cut.

Lee Honeyball in the *Observer Sports Monthly*, 6 February 2005. Clijsters and Hewitt are no longer an item.

Lindsay is the ... slightly Waspish schoolmarm, who might have taught Anne of Green Gables to read, write and sew.
Matthew Norman in the *Evening Standard*, 4 July 2005.

Jaroslav Drobny

Drobny brought to Centre Court a hint of arrogance and a distinct whiff of formaldehyde.
Lew Hoad on the the Czech-born player (and world-renowned taxidermist) who reached the Wimbledon men's singles final in 1954.

He defeated Rosewall in the 1954 final despite having been up till four in the morning mounting a hippopotamus at the Natural History Museum.

Now that *is* class. Harry Pearson in the *Guardian*, 25 June 2005.

Roger Federer

Describing Federer's defeat by the piratically trousered teenage sensation Rafael Nadal in the semi-final of the 2005 French Open:
Federer yielded to Nadal like a gazelle rolling over in the Serengeti dust before a lion.
Matthew Norman in the *Evening Standard*, 31 June 2005.

The only black mark against Roger Federer is that he looks a bit like Quentin Tarantino.

Anon. Centre Court spectator after a near-flawless Federer defeated Andy Roddick to win his third successive Wimbledon title, 3 July 2005.

Maybe I'll just punch him or something before we go on court next time.

Andy Roddick speculates on how to beat Federer after his Wimbledon men's final thumping by the Swiss, 3 July 2005.

Brad Gilbert

Gilbert, you don't deserve to be on the same court with me!

John McEnroe to Gilbert at change-over in the Masters Cup, 1986; quoted by Tim Adams in *Being John McEnroe* (2004).

You are the worst! The fucking worst!

McEnroe, facing defeat in the same match, to Gilbert again.

Justin Gimelstob

Gimelstob sounds a little like an American beer that did not quite make it; as a tennis player he is much the same.

Paul Weaver on a US player who once said of himself, 'I used to be a psycho'; in the *Guardian*, 25 June 2005.

Tim Henman — nice-but-no-Wimbledon

Describing Henman's demise in the 2005 Australian Open:

Timothy Henman yielded himelf to Nikolai Davidenko with a passivity suggesting the wedding night of a 19th-century ex-nun with lesbian leanings.
Matthew Norman in the *Evening Standard*, 31 January 2005.

The human equivalent of beige.
Comedian Linda Smith.

When he plays the court is dotted with mumsy women carrying mascots and wearing silly hats.

Justin Cartwright in the *Evening Standard*, 24 June 2005.

Soon Henman Hill will be renamed Murray Mound, the crazed spinsters will take their carnal fantasies back to their rural villages and the Henman parents will remove their long, expressionless faces from the players' box for the last time.
Matthew Norman predicts Murray's rise and Henman's fall; in the *Evening Standard*, 20 June 2005.

After watching Henman's five-set first-round victory against Jarkko Nieminen at Wimbledon 2005:

He was a bit pathetic today but I suppose he's a national treasure really.

Anon. inhabitant of Henman Hill; quoted by Stephen Bierley in the *Guardian*, 22 June 2005.

… a buttoned-up Home Counties bore unable to conjure sufficient devil to win at the highest level.

Paul Kelso in the *Guardian*, 22 June 2005.

… stiff and expressionless as shop window dummies overdosed on Botox.

Matthew Norman on Henman's parents; in the *Evening Standard*, 27 June 2005.

He walks round the court … like a straight bloke in a gay pub walking up to the bar to get the drinks in. Manly, very manly.

Chris Maume in the *Independent*, 25 June 2005.

Describing Henman's expletive-ridden second-round exit from Wimbledon 2005:

… even tennis can bring out a man's inner Rooney.

Giles Smith in *The Times*, 24 June 2005. At one point in his defeat by Dmitry Tursunov Henman fumed: 'Tell them [the ballboys] to get their heads out of their arses and bring me a coke.'

Gimelstob dived so much that Jürgen Klinsmann would have been jealous.
Paul Weaver on Gimelstob's spectacular diving during a match with Lleyton Hewitt, Wimbledon 2005.

Ivo Karlovic

Croatia leads the world in the production of elongated tennis players. Karlovic is 6ft 10in, Ivan Ljubicic is 6ft 4in. What's going on over there? Some kind of national stretching programme?
Giles Smith in *The Times*, 30 June 2005.

Anna Kournikova

Her entire career might have been termed a storm in a D-Cup.
Rick Broadbent, 'Sold on Sharapova', in *The Times*, 20 June 2005.

Svetlana Kuznetsova

… built like the Kremlin.
BBC commentary, Wimbledon 2005, on the hefty Russian.

Feliciano López

It is no good looking like a Greek statue if you move like one.
Paul Weaver in the *Guardian*, 30 June 2005, as the Spaniard freezes in his Wimbledon quarter-final against Lleyton Hewitt.

John McEnroe

Runt.

McEnroe's nickname when he played in his school's basketball team, bestowed on account of his relatively diminutive size.

I'm so disgusting that you shouldn't watch. Everybody leave!

McEnroe to the crowd at the Queen's club, 1981.

Responding to the question 'Have you and Stacey [McEnroe's then girlfriend] split up':

I'd like you to quote that you guys are shit.

McEnroe, press conference after his 1981 Wimbledon semi-final victory over Rod Frawley.

I remember a poll in a Miami paper to find the worst people of all time. Charles Manson was one, Attila the Hun was two, I was three and Jack the Ripper was four.

McEnroe interviewed by Brian Viner in the *Independent*, 20 June 2005.

McEnroe has the wiry frame and whiney drawl of Woody Allen on steroids.

Rick Broadbent in *The Times*, 29 June 2005.

I'm more competitive than the average bear.
McEnroe on playing the Seniors tour, quoted on bbc.co.uk.

On being advised 'don't ever change' by his showbusiness friends at
the time of his being banned from the Davis Cup:
**When you're 26, who are you gonna listen to –
Jagger and Nicholson or some old farts in the
United States Tennis Association?**
McEnroe, quoted by Tim Adams in *Being John McEnroe* (2004).

Amélie Mauresmo

Half a man – because she has a girlfriend.
An enlightened observation from Martina Hingis, shortly before the
'Swiss Miss' defeated Mauresmo in the 1999 Australian Open final.

Andrew Murray

**… a sort of hangdog version of John Gordon
Sinclair in *Gregory's Girl* … highly entertaining in a
Kevin the teenager sort of way off the lawns.**
Ian Chadband in the *Evening Standard*, 24 June 2005.

**It might be time to change the slang term for a
curry: from a Ruby Murray to an Andy Murray.**
Brian Viner in the *Independent*, 24 June 2005. Murray achieved his
second-round Wimbledon victory over 14th seed Radek Stepanek
despite suffering the effects of a chicken curry eaten the night before.

The jaw-dropping grimace that accompanies his yells of triumph, while refreshingly un-Henmanesque in its gurning vehemence, suggests the agonized reaction of a man who has just had a sharp object introduced into his back passage.

Anon. tennis journalist on the new young hopeful of British tennis, June 2005.

Anastasia Myskina

The raven-haired Russian is a puzzle wrapped in an enigma with a decent forehand sellotaped to the exterior of the package.

Andrew Baker in the *Daily Telegraph*, 29 June 2005.

Rafael Nadal

... the No. 4 seed arrived on court looking like Johnny Depp in *Pirates of the Caribbean*.

Robert Philip is impressed by Nadal's three-quarter-length *pantalones* (or are they clam diggers? or Capri pants?); in the *Daily Telegraph*, 24 May 2005.

Leyton Hewitt — tennis's Jimmy Porter

It's difficult to love Lleyton, but he's all we've got.
Tennis commentator Chris Bradman quotes an Australian
newspaper, quoted by Chris Maume in the *Independent*, 29
January 2005. Maume added, 'for different reasons, the
English feel the same way about Tim Henman (Canadians
don't count).'

Safin recovered from a hideous start not merely to dominate Hewitt but to crush the spirit out of the odious little git.

Matthew Norman exults at Marat Safin's defeat of Hewitt in the
2005 Australian Open final; *Evening Standard*, 31 January 2005.

**Apparently he's accepted the cameo role as a
tranvestite sheep-shearer in a new movie, *Meet the
Ockers*.**
Matthew Norman puns at Hewitt's expense on the title of
the movie *Meet the Fockers*.

Not the first time the words 'Hewitt' and 'freak' have appeared in the same sentence.

The *Guardian* selects Hewitt ('groggy Aussie') for its 'performance of the week', 21 May 2005 after a mysterious 'household accident' left him nursing a cracked rib and ruled him out of the French Open.

... intense and chippy, like a pit-bull terrier ... This is tennis's Jimmy Porter, who looks not only back but forwards and sideways in anger.

Paul Weaver in the *Guardian*, 27 June 2005.

... this little harbour tug-boat of a man among the supertankers at the top of world tennis.

Richard Edmondson in the *Independent*, 25 June 2005.

Depending on your point of view, Hewitt is either a paradigm of Antipodean pluck, a celebration of the combative spark which lies dormant in most human beings, or a complete pillock.

Richard Edmondson.

There are players who make tennis look easy and Hewitt is not among them ... In Hewitt's blue-collar version of the game, the wiring and the plumbing are visible.

Giles Smith in *The Times*, 30 June 2005.

The baseball cap worn back to front makes him resemble a redneck petrol pump attendant.

'Match Points', in *The Times*, 30 June 2005.

Imagine the love-child of Jimmy Connors and the young Mike Tyson…

Matthew Norman in the *Evening Standard*, 31 June 2005, after the 19-year-old Mallorcan had defeated Argentina's Mariano Puerta to win the French Open title.

David Nalbandian

The man who shot Bambi.

Paul Newman in the *Independent*, 28 June 2005, alluding to the Argentinian's five-set defeat of the teenaged Scot Andrew Murray in the third round of Wimbledon 2005.

Ilie Nastase

Ace me and I'll pull my pants down.

Nastase to Gene Mayer in the 2005 Wimbledon veterans' event. He was as good as his word.

Mark Philippoussis

… once a Scud and now the size of a B52 bomber.

Alan Fraser in the *Daily Mail*, 23 June 2005, reporting the demise of a bulky Philippoussis in the face of an onslaught by Marat Safin.

Mary Pierce

Scary Mary.
Nickname for the powerful Pierce in the mid-1990s.

It would be unfair to call Pierce a basket case. She is too elegant for that. She is more like a Prada handbag case...
Sue Mott in the *Daily Telegraph*, 29 June 2005.

Dr Renée Richards

How hungry must you be for tennis success to have your penis cut off?
John Aizlewood, 'The top ten sporting name changes' in the *Sunday Times*, 13 February 2005. Richard Raskind, eye surgeon and useful tennis player, had a sex-change operation in 1975. As Renée Richards, she became a professional on the women's tour, reaching the quarter-finals of the US Open in 1978 and later coaching Martina Navratilova.

Andy Roddick

The American is reliant on two weapons ... his serve and his forehand ... Once either of these shots malfunctions he is plain and his attempts at variety, notably on the serve and volley, are cringingly awful.
Stephen Bierley in the *Guardian*, 29 Janauary 2005.

On the American's appearance after his five-set victory over Daniele Bracciale at Wimbledon 2005:
The reversed white baseball cap called to mind a number of images (none of them close to Wimbledon champion) – asylum inmate, *sous-chef*, First World War shell-shock victim...
Anon. journalist, 24 June 2005.

After Roddick's pasting by Roger Federer in the 2005 Wimbledon final:
Alas, poor Roddick, we wished him well.
Kevin Geary, BBC1 News, 3 July 2005.

On grass he has the identical chance of defeating Federer as does Stephen Hawking.
Matthew Norman in the *Evening Standard*, 4 July 2005.

Marat Safin

Safin is slightly bananas in the grand Yeltsinian manner – after winning the 2000 US Open title he went on a three-year bender...

Matthew Norman in the *Evening Standard*, 31 January 2005.

... he has about as much connection with grass as a broken lawnmower.

Leo Spall and Raoul Simons as Safin loses to Feliciano López at Wimbledon 2005; in the *Evening Standard*, 24 June 2005.

Monica Seles

Camel noises.

Apt anagram of the name of the greatest grunter of the pre-Sharapova era (*see also* page 293).

Maria Sharapova

Sharapova has lived so long in Florida that she sounds like one of those high-octane weather girls for CNN.

Martin Johnson in the *Daily Telegraph*, 28 January 2005.

… she is exactly like Kournikova, apart from having a better double-handed backhand. Like the legendary Russian coquette, Sharapova has used her looks to plunder a raft of endorsements … Kournikova did this by saying 'My breasts look really good because they don't sag.' Sharapova has done this by winning tournaments and, unwittingly, by fuelling schoolboy fantasies.

Rick Broadbent, 'Sold on Sharapova', in *The Times*, 20 June 2005.

You are left in no doubt by the 18-year-old Wimbledon champion that you are in the presence of greatness every time she swaggers into the press room. Until, that is, she opens her mouth to speak – then the greatness descends into a dreary monotone.

David McVay watches the Eastern Europeans at the DFS Classic at Edgbaston, in *The Times*, 20 June 2005.

… the truth of the matter is that Sharapova is not beautiful. You could find 100 prettier faces in the audience …

Simon Barnes points out the truth about Maria; in *The Times*, 23 June 2005.

How do you quieten a grunter like Maria?

... the grunting and screaming reached the kind of decibel level that might have prompted a raid from the Melbourne vice squad.

Martin Johnson on Maria Sharapova during her Australian Open semi-final defeat by Serena Williams, in the *Daily Telegraph*, 28 January 2005.

... louder than a pneumatic drill and only nine decibels less than a plane taking off.

Shektar Bhatia in the *Evening Standard*, 21 June 2005, as Sharapova breaks the Wimbledon all-comers' record with an extraordinary grunt of 101.2 decibels.

Sharapova has an impressive vocal range: with several different kinds of grunt. Occasionally she shrieked, occasionally she let out a low bass note of a grunt, occasionally she attempted to muffle the noise, and occasionally she really went for it and came close to stripping the paint off the Debentures Enclosure.

Mark Hodgkinson on Sharapova's grunting in her Wimbledon 2005 match with fellow-Russian Nadia Petrova, 'Queen of screams ups tempo', in the *Daily Telegraph*, 29 June 2005.

Imagine Maria Sharapova on a hen night in Newcastle. With her willowy frame she'd not last five minutes before collapsing under the weight of the flashing 'Sperm Donor Wanted' novelty headgear.

Harry Pearson in the *Guardian*, 25 June 2005.

Sharapova grunt comparisons

the top four

... a Billingsgate costermonger.
Jim White in the *Daily Telegraph*, 29 June 2005.

... the noise an owl might make were you to hit it hard with a stick.
Giles Smith in *The Times*, 29 June 2005.

... a barking muntjak.
Caller to BBC Radio Five Live. (A muntjak is a small deer now widespread in, though not native to, the UK.)

... a live pig being slaughtered.
Frew MacMillan, BBC Radio Five Live.

Jeff Tarango

Society will accept you if you are a jerk and win.
Jeff Tarango's father, quoted by Harry Pearson in the *Guardian*, 20 June 2005. Tarango *fils* probably belonged more in the non-winning jerk category. During a third-round match at Wimbledon in 1995 he notoriously called French umpire Bruno Rebeuh 'the most corrupt official in the game' before stomping off without finishing the match. Tarango's French wife Bénédicte then added injury to insult by slapping the hapless Rebeuh when he came off court. Tarango was disqualified, fined £30,000 and banned from two grand slam tournaments.

Serena Williams

Her movement around the court … put one in mind of a woman in a panty girdle and high heels running for a bus.
Martin Johnson on Serena Williams against Maria Sharapova in the Australian Open semi-final, in the *Daily Telegraph*, 28 January 2005.

My balls felt good today.
Serena Williams examines herself during the Australian Open, 29 January 2005, quoted on sportal.com.au.

… her breasts alone must weigh more than Justine
Henin-Hardenne.
Matthew Norman in the *Evening Standard*, 27 June 2005, following
a palpably overweight Serena's third-round Wimbledon defeat by the
obscure Jill Craybas (*see* page 276).

… next to [Serena Williams] Jordan seems a
candidate for a trainer bra.
Matthew Norman in the *Evening Standard*, 4 July 2005.

Venus Williams

Venus does less bling than her sister and that includes grand slam trophies.

Sue Mott in the *Daily Telegraph*, 29 June 2005.

Williams doesn't grunt. She roars. It's a tigerish snarl rather than a loud exhalation. Most female players grunt in a vaguely copulatory fashion. The sound of Venus in full cry is not so much venereal as martial.

Simon Barnes in *The Times*, 29 June 2005.

On Venus's chances of winning Wimbledon 2005:

There is more chance of Serena Williams becoming Ms Flat Chested USA.

Matthew Norman gets it completely wrong; in the *Evening Standard*, June 2005.

● WOMEN'S TENNIS
something -ovic and somebody -okova

... the grunting and gasping make tense rallies sound like the diner scene in *When Harry Met Sally*.
Harry Pearson in the *Guardian*, 20 June 2005.

The only requirements for full prodigy status are having a Barbie and a faintly sociopathic parent.
Rick Broadbent in *The Times*, 20 June 2005.

... [women's tennis] seems to be a Nike-based *Stepford Wives* for kids.
Rick Broadbent.

Cloned baseline brats.
David McVay on the new generation of baseline-favouring Eastern European women players, in *The Times*, 20 June 2005.

From a distance, it was impossible to distinguish between one something -ovic with long legs and long blonde hair and another somebody -okova with similar body parts.
David McVay watches the Eastern Europeans at the DFS Classic at Edgbaston.

● WIMBLEDON
it's a little bit pervy

You have put sin and vulgarity into tennis.
Anon. Wimbledon committee member to Teddy Tinling; quoted by Harry Pearson in the *Guardian*, 20 June 2005. Tinling designed the famous lace-trimmed panties worn by 'Gorgeous Gussie' Moran at Wimbledon in 1949, and, according to Tim Adams in *Being John McEnroe* (2004) '… he … pandered to Middle England's underwear fetishists by becoming knickers-supplier to the stars'. Press photographers have been taking worm's-eye shots of women tennis players' knickers ever since.

There is something pervy about Wimbledon crowds that gather for matches involving a Sharapova, a Hantuchova or a Dokic.
Rick Broadbent in *The Times*, 20 June 2005.

The Australian Open

An event that used to be such an irrelevance that John Lloyd once made the final.
Matthew Norman in the *Evening Standard*, 31 January 2005.

Tennis Rule No. 1: no one cares about the Australian Open.
Chris Maume in the *Independent*, 29 January 2005.

Two things Dan Maskell *actually* said

The Gullikson twins here. An interesting pair, both from Wisconsin.

Lendl has remained throughout as calm as the proverbial iceberg.

We haven't had any more rain since it stopped raining.

Harry Carpenter, BBC commentary.

Two things Dan Maskell *never said*

I am sure, like me, you long to have those long, moist, Russian legs wrapped round your face.
Mock the Week, BBC TV, June 2005.

All this grunting is giving me the horn.
Mock the Week, BBC TV, June 2005.

On the former British No. 5 and successor to Dan Maskell in the Wimbledon commentary box:

In more than three decades of talking about tennis, John Barrett has failed to utter one phrase that stays in the mind.
Will Buckley in the *Observer*, 30 January 2005.

Wimbledon is the sexiest tournament of them all because of its primness, because of its feeling that all the time the chaperone is lurking round the corner. At Wimbledon, it feels as if we have got away with something.
Simon Barnes in *The Times*, 23 June 2005.

GOLF

Boulevard of broken dreams

Excessive golfing dwarfs the intellect. Nor is this to be wondered at when we consider that the more fatuously vacant the mind is, the better for play. It has been observed that absolute idiots play the steadiest.
Sir Walter Simpson, *The Art of Golf* (1887).

Golf is the cruellest of sports. Like life, it's unfair. It's a harlot. A trollop. It leads you on. It never lives up to its promises … It's a boulevard of broken dreams. It plays with men. And runs off with the butcher.
Jim Murray.

Give me the fresh air, a beautiful partner, and a nice round of golf … and you can keep the fresh air and the round of golf.
Jack Benny.

I'd give up golf if I didn't have so many sweaters.
Bob Hope.

In primitive society, when native tribes beat the ground with clubs and yelled, it was called witchcraft; today, in civilized society, it is called golf.
Anon.

The US Open

The only remarkable thing about our national championship is how consistently the USGA manages to snatch ennui from the jaws of excitement.
Michael Corcoran, 'The Open's the Worst', on golfonline.com, June 2004.

Golf is an open exhibition of overweening ambition, courage deflated by stupidity, skill scoured by a whiff of arrogance.
Alistair Cooke.

Golf appeals to the idiot in us and the child. Just how childlike golf players become is proven by their frequent inability to count past five.
John Updike.

The people who gave us golf and called it a game are the same people who gave us bagpipes and called it music.
US TV show *Silk Stockings*.

Golf is cow-pasture pool.
O.K. Bovard.

The Open

Only the British Open can get away with its annual aesthetic torture, staging the thing in places that have no beauty, no style, no landscaping. Plant a geranium, for cripe's sake.

Bernie Lincicome, *Rocky Mountain News*, on the selection of Royal St. George's, Sandwich, for the 2003 British Open. (Note to Bernie: Britons were world-class gardeners when Bobby Jones's manicured Georgia lawns were wilderness roamed by hunter-gatherers.)

Any society that puts such an extraordinary price on a trivial pursuit such as golf ... needs to pause for a moment and consider where it is going wrong.

Carol Murray of the Scottish Low Pay Unit on the revelation that it can cost up to £100,000 for a member of the public to play a round of golf with top players such as Ernie Els, Retief Goossen, Sergio Garcia and John Daly; quoted in the *Guardian*, 11 March 2005.

The reason most people play golf is to wear clothes they would not be caught dead in otherwise.

Roger Simon.

Darren Clarke

Darren Clarke Syndrome (inexplicable affection for dodgy trousers).
Bill Elliott in the *Observer*, 10 July 2005.

Ben Crenshaw

I'm about five inches from being an outstanding golfer. That's the distance my left ear is from my right.
Ben Crenshaw. Bobby Jones, founder of the Masters tournament, once remarked: 'Golf is a game that is played on a five-inch course – the distance between your ears.'

John Daly

I like to eat all the shit you're not supposed to eat.
John Daly, quoted in the *Evening Standard*, 7 April 2005. Daly commented in June 2005: 'I've got the drinkers and the smokers and the eaters on my side. They like what I do.'

Everyone's favourite redneck.
Gavin Newsham in the *Guardian*, 25 June 2005.

See also Nick Faldo (page 309).

Luke Donald

Luke Donald has a great chance, the way he plods along.
Tiger Woods assesses the form before the US Open at Pinehurst, quoted in the *Guardian*, 16 June 2005.

David Duval

Best contact you've made all year, Duval.
Nike advert poking fun at Duval's demise as a golfer. In it he leads a group of golfers messing around in Tiger Woods's garage. After rummaging through a golf bag, Duval takes a practice swing and smashes a car window. An animated head cover looks up and says the above.

How to use a 1-iron

If you're caught on a golf course during a storm and are afraid of lightning, hold up a 1-iron. Not even God can hit a 1-iron.
Lee Trevino.

Nick Faldo

Describing 'Wild Thing' John Daly:

John certainly gives it a good hit, doesn't he? My Sunday best is a Wednesday afternoon compared to him.
Nick Faldo.

Socially a 24-handicapper.
Faldo's second wife Jill Bennett, 1995, the year her two-year marriage to Faldo ended; quoted in the *Observer Sports Monthly*, February 2005.

Fred Funk

Funk is 48 years old going on 12.
Lawrence Donegan in the *Guardian*, 30 March 2005.

Retief Goosen

Golf's answer to Inspector Clouseau.
David Facey in the *Sun*, 18 February 2005, after Goosen got himself thrown out of the £4 million Nissan Open for oversleeping and missing the curtain-raising pro-am event before the tournament itself.

As patient as a saint, as relentless as a waterfall.
John Hopkins quotes a press judgement of the undemonstrative South African, in the *Independent*, 20 June 2005.

… Goosen … must be the dullest character in sport.
Matthew Norman in the *Evening Standard*, 20 June 2005.

Colin Montgomerie

A physique made for roll-neck jumpers and the natural bonhomie of a rainy parade.
Rick Broadbent in *The Times*, 18 July 2005.

When it comes to body language he is the unabridged Oxford dictionary, in a dozen volumes.
Richard Williams in the *Guardian*, 18 July 2005.

Warning golf can seriously diminish your balls

The sport of choice for the urban poor is basketball. The sport of choice for maintenance level employees is bowling. The sport of choice for front-line workers is football. The sport of choice for supervisors is baseball. The sport of choice for middle management is tennis. The sport of choice for corporate officers is golf. Conclusion: the higher you are in the corporate structure, the smaller your balls become.
Anon.

How to use a sand wedge

Real golfers, no matter what the provocation, never strike a caddie with the driver. The sand wedge is far more effective.
Huxtable Pippey.

A nearly man who will remain in the file marked 'underachiever'.
Rick Broadbent.

Monty was born with 10,000 volts running through him.
Martin Johnson in the *Daily Telegraph*, 18 July 2005.

Jack Nicklaus

The only interesting thing about the retirement of Jack Nicklaus at the ... Open at St Andrews on Friday is why it didn't happen long ago ... has-beens like Nicklaus clutter up the golf circuit, denying vital opportunities to younger talent.
Peter Oborne in the *Evening Standard*, 18 July 2005.

The ultimate handicap

Replying to a spectator at the Masters golf tournament who asked him what his handicap was:

Congress.
US President Lyndon Johnson.

Jesper Parnevik

I think I'm the first [player] to ever come here having left their clubs in the garage.
The eccentric Swede arrives at Augusta from his Florida home for the 2005 Masters.

Lee Trevino

My swing is so bad I look like a caveman killing his lunch.
Lee Trevino.

I'm not saying my golf game went bad, but if I grew tomatoes, they'd come up sliced.
Lee Trevino.

One under a tree, one under a bush, one under the water.
Trevino, standing at one under during a tournament, analyses his round.

Lee Westwood

I'm a golfer, not an athlete.
Westwood on himself.

Tiger Woods

Fifty years ago, 100 white men chasing one black man across a field was called the Ku Klux Klan. Today it's called the PGA Tour.
Anon.

[Woods has the] disrespectful and rather distasteful habit of depositing dollops of phlegm all over hallowed venues at seemingly every available opportunity. Great expectorations indeed.
John Huggan in the *Guardian*, 21 June 2005.

Q: What do Tiger Woods and his blonde fiancée have in common?

A: They both have black roots.
Internet joke, c.2004.

On Woods and his Swedish supermodel wife, Elin Nordegren:
The last time I saw so plastic-looking a pair was in two boxes marked 'Ken' and 'Barbie'.
Anon. journalist.

Woods ... may well be an android from an alien planet who landed here in a spacecraft and who occasionally loses tournaments on purpose so people won't suspect.
Martin Johnson in the *Daily Telegraph,* 18 July 2005.

US SPORT

Who are they trying to kid?

I used to consider American sport to be an introspective, nationalistic joke. Super Bowl, World Championships, World Series – who were these Yanks trying to kid? No wonder an American team won; only Americans played their damned sports.

Ed Smith in *Playing Hard Ball* (2002).

● RUGBY LEAGUE WITH KNOBS ON
American Football

Football? Hell, what is it? It's a sick game – a whole lot of guys trying to beat the crap out of one another. If I could play golf just as well, I'd do it.
American footballer Jim McMahon.

Football is not a contact sport. It's a collision sport. Dancing is a good example of a contact sport.
Duffy Daugherty, football coach, in *Sports Illustrated*, 14 October 1963.

There are several differences between a football game and a revolution. For one thing, a football game usually lasts longer and the participants wear uniforms. Also, there are usually more casualties in a football game … Kicking is very important in football. In fact, some of the more enthusiastic players even kick the ball occasionally.
Alfred Hitchcock, British film director.

If the Super Bowl is the 'Ultimate Game', why are they playing it again next year?
Duane Thomas, American footballer.

American football is not so much a sport as a way of strife. It might be best described as rugby league with knobs on, or feinting by numbers.
Doug Ibbertson, British sportswriter, *Sporting Scenes* (1980).

College football today is one of the last great strongholds of genuine old-fashioned American hypocrisy.
Paul Gallico, US journalist and author, *Farewell to Sport* (1938).

Football brings out the sociologist that lurks in some otherwise respectable citizens.
George Will, *The Pursuit of Happiness and Other Sobering Thoughts*, 1978.

On sacking his manager:
I gave George Allen an unlimited budget and he exceeded it.
Club owner Edward B. Williams.

● BASEBALL
'wild times and rampant 'roids'

There's no skill involved. Just go up there and swing at the ball.
Joe DiMaggio.

It's like watching grass – no, Astro Turf – grow.
Jeff Jarvis in *Entertainment Weekly*, 1990.

Summing up the standard British view of baseball:
… a typically populist and vulgar American bastardization of a minor English game played by girls.
Cricketing baseball fan Ed Smith in his *Playing Hard Ball* (2002).

Babe Ruth

A drunkard, a glutton and a hellraiser.
Ed Smith on the man known variously as 'the sultan of swat, the wali of wallop, and wazie of wham, the maharajah of mash, rajah of rap, the caliph of clout and the behemoth of bust', in *Playing Hard Ball* (2002).

Jose Canseco

Baseball's slimeball.

Headline in the *Evening Standard*, 22 February 2005. In his book *Juiced: Wild Times, Rampant 'Roids, Smash Hits and How Baseball Got Big*, former baseball star Canseco made claims of widespread and systematic use of performance-enhancing drugs in the sport and predicted a time when a majority of athletes in all sports will take steroids: 'And believe it or not, that's good news.'

Jose is an attention-grabbing crackpot with the credibility of a street-corner snitch.

Bryan Burwell of the *St Louis Post Despatch*, quoted in the *Evening Standard*, 22 February 2005.

George Steinbrenner

Nobody *wants* to do a Steinbrenner chapter. You go into the book thinking to yourself, 'I don't want to give that overbloated bag of bile any more ink than he's already gotten.'

Kevin Nelson, quoted in *Baseball's Even Greater Insults* (1993); on George Steinbrenner, owner of the New York Yankees since 1973.

George doesn't know a fucking thing about the game of baseball. That's the bottom line.

Dallas Green, manager in 1989.

On New York Yankees' manager Stump Merrill being described as 'the apple of George Steinbrenner's eye':

Sooner or later, of course, being the apple of his eye is the same as being the apple of William Tell's eye.

Dave Anderson.

Baseball pitchers

throwing, throwing and ... throwing

The pitchers sometimes look like the kind of guys that the beefcake hitters might beat up in their spare time.

Ed Smith in *Playing Hard Ball* (2002).

If we eliminated pitchers they wouldn't be missed: they are pampered little swine with no real effect on the game except dragging it out and interrupting the action.

US satirical magazine.

The first thing you have to understand about pitchers is they're non-athletes. All they can do is throw. That's the whole athletic package. Throwing, throwing and throwing.

New York Mets' hitter Todd Zeile on pitchers.

Respecting Mister Asshole

– You asshole!

– What'd you call me?

– An asshole.

– Listen, buddy, I've got more years in the bigs then you've been alive. How about showing some respect?

– All right. *Mister* Asshole.

Pleasantries exchanged between the young Dodgers infielder Adam Peterson and veteran pitcher Jerry Reuss, after the latter had hit the former on the leg with a ball.

When I was a little boy, I wanted to be a baseball player and join the circus. With the Yankees I've accomplished both.

Baseman Graig Nettles, one-time apple of Steinbrenner's eye.

Describing the day Steinbrenner was banned from baseball (briefly, as it turned out) for paying fraudster Howie Spira $40,000 to 'get dirt' on one of his own players, outfielder Dave Winfield:

July 30th may become a patriotic holiday in New York City and wherever the proud traditions of baseball are honoured.

Time magazine, 1990.

● BASKETBALL
a fascination with soaring armpits

The invention of basketball was not an accident. It was developed to meet a need. Those boys simply would not play 'Drop the Handkerchief'.
Dr James Naismith, the man credited with the invention of basketball.

Nothing there but basketball, a game which won't be fit for people until they set the basket umbilicus-high and return the giraffes to the zoo.
Ogden Nash, US poet and humorist.

Many Americans follow pro basketball from November through June, for reasons that I found unexplainable, other than the fact that they were overly fascinated with soaring armpits.
Dan Jenkins, *You Call It Sports...* (1989).

I sight down my nose to shoot, and now my nose isn't straight since I broke it. That's why my shooting has been off.
Barrie Haynie, US basketball player.

I'll always remember this as the night Michael and I combined to score 70 points.

US basketball player Stacey King. Michael Jordan scored 69 of them.

The team is boring and lifeless. For over 20 years the Boston Celtics have stood for something. The only thing they stand for now is the anthem.

Bob Ryan in the *Boston Globe*.

George McGinnis has got the body of a Greek god and the running ability of a Greek goddess.

Dick Vitale, US basketball player.

The Atlanta Hawks are a bunch of guys who would prefer to pass kidney stones than pass a basketball.

Bob Weiss, US basketball coach.

OTHER SPORTS
(mostly minor ones)

● ATHLETICS
gurning into a head wind

Kelly Holmes

Kelly Holmes' outfit on Sunday looked like
something a transvestite builder might favour.
Matthew Norman on the dress Holmes wore for the BBC TV
sports personality of the year awards; in the *Evening Standard*,
17 December 2004.

Steve Ovett

... all elbows and bared teeth, like a mobile gurner
struggling in a head wind.
Stuart Jeffries in the *Guardian*, 14 July 2005.

Great moments in Olympic history 1

To King Gustav V of Sweden after the Swedish monarch
told him 'You, sir, are the greatest athlete in the world' at
the medal ceremony at the 1912 Stockholm Olympics:

Thanks, King.
US athlete Jim Thorpe.

Paula Radcliffe

She has become a tormented character from, fittingly enough, Greek myth, lumbered with the Sisyphean curse of forever pushing the weight of self-expectation towards the peak, never reaching it.

Matthew Norman on the post-Athens Paula; in the *Evening Standard*, 18 April 2005.

The most excruciatingly embarrassing pit-stop in the history of the sport.

Ian Chadband on Radcliffe's 'comfort break' during the 2005 London Marathon; in the *Evening Standard*, 18 April 2005.

Paula Radcliffe, so much more than just a jobbing athlete.

Anon sports journalist, c.2004.

Spend a penny, earn a million dollars.

The *Guardian*, 18 April 2005.

They should mark the spot with a brown plaque.

Anon. wag, quoted by Ian Chadband in the *Evening Standard*, 18 April 2005.

Crouching Paula, hidden drama.
Ian Chadband.

She's a very good runner, but her guts – in every
sense – leave something to be desired.
Piers Morgan in the *Evening Standard*, 19 April 2005.

One woman pees in the street, another vomits
copiously. So, a typical Sunday on the streets of
your average British city.
Bob Horne, letter to the *Guardian*, 19 April 2005.

Great moments in Olympic history 2

Et maintenant, un moment historique pour la France…
French TV commentator, the moment before the
announcement that London would host the 2012 Olympic
Games, July 2005.

First John of Arc and now this.
A Parisian hotel doorman reacts to the news that London
will stage the 2012 Olympics; quoted by Bernie Lincicome,
Rocky Mountain News, 7 July 2005.

● BOWLS
bastion of conservatism

Bowls … is a bastion of conservatism straight
from the novels of Angus Wilson, with members
dressing up in tennis outfits circa 1930.
Matthew Syed in *The Times*, 7 June 2005.

Glitz and Tits.
Nickname accorded the so-
called 'Bowls Babe' Carol
Ashby, world indoor bowls
champion in mixed pairs, by
size-18 Scottish bowls player
Linda Brennan. Ashby caused
something of a stir in the staid world
of bowls by virtue of her 'allegedly voracious
sexual appetite, breast implants, tattoos and piercings'
(Matthew Syed in *The Times*, 7 June 2005).

● BOXING
whacking 'bums'

Joe Calzaghe

This Welsh boxer has whacked more bums than 'Professor' Jimmy Edwards.

Matthew Norman in the *Evening Standard*, 9 May 2005.

Howard Eastman

You should be scared. You are looking at one hell of a mean motherfucker.

Bernard Hopkins (self-styled 'Executioner') to Howard Eastman before their world middleweight bout, quoted in the *Sun*, 18 February 2005.

Naseem Hamed

… excuse me if I pull my punches today in considering the cocky little git's proposed comeback.

Matthew Norman, 'Fat chance I'll be cheering on Naz', in the *Evening Standard*, 7 February 2005.

Kevin McBride

I'm going to gut him like a fish. He's just a tomato can.

Mike Tyson on the 'Clones Colossus', June 2005. The overweight Irishman beat Tyson in six rounds, ending the career of the 'baddest man on the planet'. Tyson remarked after the defeat: 'No disrespect to Kevin, but if I can't beat him, I can't beat Junior Jones [a former world bantamweight and superbantamweight champion].'

Mike Tyson

Tyson, I love you, you're the only guy I know who's made a bigger mess of his life than me.

Truck driver to Tyson at a red light, recalled by Tyson and quoted by John Lawton in *The Independent*, 9 June 2005.

After his defeat by Kevin McBride:

I'm a cruel and cold and hard person. I've been abused in every way you can imagine. Save your tears. I lost my sensitivity. You embarrass me when you cry.

Tyson to assembled journalists; quoted in *The Times*, 13 June 2005.

A rapist once voted BBC overseas sports personality of the year.

Owen Slot in *The Times*, 13 June 2005.

● DARTS
whippets and tubs of lard

Andy Fordham

Known as 'The Viking'. Gargantuan darts champion with roadkill on his head. On closer examination, the roadkill appears to be a hairstyle. The nation shudders when he appears on *Celebrity Fit Club*.
William Donaldson and Hermione Eyre, *The Dictionary of National Celebrity* (2005).

I used to be called the whippet
The 30-stone Fordham on himself, quoted on bbc.co.uk.

On Fordham's retirement from his match with Phil Taylor due to heat exhaustion:
The wake-up call every 30-stone tub of lard needs.
Chris Maume in the *Independent*, 29 January 2005.

Sid Waddell

The drinking man's Alan Bennett.
The Rough Guide to Cult Football (2003).

● FORMULA ONE
a waste of good champagne

Grand prix racing is like balancing an egg on a spoon while shooting the rapids.
Graham Hill, quoted in the *Guardian*, 11 July 2005.

I have always tended to the view that the whole business is more or less a waste of good champagne.
Martin Kelner in the *Guardian*, 7 March 2005.

… some vast and private Scalextric set for megalomaniac millionaires.
Paul Weaver in the *Guardian*, 9 July 2005.

Describing those for whom Formula One is not the sport of viewing choice:
… [they] would rather watch an unusually dismal Am Dram society perform King Lear in a Walsall community centre than the average race.
Matthew Norman in the *Evening Standard*, 20 June 2005.

… as much spectator appeal as the G8 conference.
Paul Weaver on the 2005 US grand prix at Indianapolis, in which only six cars took part.

Silverstone

I like visiting Silverstone – it's a reminder of what racing was like in the 1950s.
F1 supremo Bernie Ecclestone has a dig at Silverstone, 2005.

You will see more overtaking at your local zebra crossing.
Paul Weaver on the 2005 British grand prix, in the *Guardian*, 11 July 2005.

Ferrari are just too darn bling these days.
The *Guardian*'s definitive guide to the 2005 Formula One season, 28 February 2005. The guide also commented: 'Minardi are the Yeading to Ferrari's Chelsea.'

… in motor racing these days raffish 'taches are as rare as a smile on the face of Andy Robinson [the England rugby union coach]. There no longer seem to be drivers who use the phrase dolly bird, either, while the entire modern breed show a boring reluctance to go out in a spectacular fireball of baby-doll nighties and double entendre.
Harry Pearson in the *Guardian*, 5 March 2005.

Jenson Button

Button could be the biggest fly in the zippy German's overalls. Or he could be pants.
The *Guardian*'s guide to the 2005 Formula One season, 28 February 2005.

Button undone.
The Times captions a picture of Button's exit from the Canadian grand prix after 47 laps, 13 June 2005.

David Coulthard

[Coulthard looks like he borrowed the] bottom of his head from Sophie Ellis-Bextor.
The *Guardian*'s guide to the 2005 Formula One season, 28 February 2005.

Bernie Ecclestone

One of the worst features of the lizardine Formula One chief is his hair, which looks suspiciously like glued-on off-cuts from a particularly manky Persian cat.
Roger Davis, June 2004.

The little dictator with the Beatles haircut.
Paul Weaver in the *Guardian*, 9 July 2005.

James Hunt

Hunt … once made the tabloids for inadvertently peeing on Esther Rantzen during a flight from Australia, having found all the aircraft's toilets in use.

Richard Williams on the hell-raising British driver of the 1970s, in the *Guardian*, 26 January 2005.

He [had] a somewhat cavalier attitude to personal hygiene, believing that the use of deodorants masks essential odours which attract women to men.

Richard Williams.

Max Mosley

I was reading a book called *The Wisdom of Crowds*. I thought: 'If thousands of people are saying I'm a tosser, maybe they are right.'

Formula One boss Max Mosley after the fiasco at the 2005 US grand prix, in which tyre problems led to only six cars starting the race; quoted on bbc.co.uk, June 2005.

Alain Prost

Well done Mr Arnoux, that Prost is a proper little prick and had it coming.

Garage attendant to Alain Prost after René Arnoux, ignoring Renault team instructions to allow his team-mate and fellow-countryman Prost to win and thereby keep his world title chances alive, had won the 1982 French grand prix.

Kimi Raikonnen

Raikonnen should take at least one pole position – in a lap-dancing club with his trousers round his ankles. Allegedly.

The *Guardian*'s definitive guide to the 2005 Formula One season on Raikonnen's chances for the 2005 season, 28 February 2005. The reference is to an incident in which the Finn allegedly dropped his trousers in front of a line of lap dancers in a Mayfair club.

Michael Schumacher

That's sorted the little bastard.

Ayrton Senna to a team colleague after whispering words of admonishment to Schumacher before the restart of the 1992 French grand prix (the young German had earlier crashed into the Brazilian's McLaren on the first lap).

A 36-year old German with a dubious taste in leaisure wear has never won the title in the Chinese year of the rooster. We think.

The *Guardian*'s guide to the 2005 Formula One season looks hard for reasons why Schumacher might not win the 2005 drivers' championship, 28 February 2005.

Michael is the most boring world champion ever.

Eddie Irvine on BBC Radio Five Live, 9 May 2005.

Jacques Villeneuve

Is-he-grungy-cool-or-is-he-a-geek-yes-he's-a-geek.

The *Guardian*'s guide to the 2005 Formula One season, 28 February 2005.

● HORSE RACING
scurrying fellows in muddy shoes

Horse racing is often called the sport of kings. In
fact it is the sport of horses and also of little fellows
in muddy shoes and green waxed caps scurrying
round in damp marquees.

'Backpages' in the *Guardian*, 7 March 2005.

On the Cheltenham Festival:

A four-day guzzlers' gymkhana.

Frank Keating, in the *Guardian*, 11 March 2005.

Horsey girls

You never see a pretty, unattached girl on a racecourse.
But you often see positive gangs of rather unpretty
ones. They are the owners or the owners' wives and
they wear mink in all weathers and far too much make-
up. For some odd reason, I can never work out why they
always seem to be married to haulage contractors in the
North, builders in the South and farmers in the West.

Jeffrey Bernard, famously unwell diarist of the *Spectator*.

John McCririck — a bogeyman at the Ivy

John McCririck is not a man to whom I would wish to be married, even if he went the extra mile to seduce me via surgery on his breasts (in his case, of course, a reduction).
Matthew Norman in the *Evening Standard*, 17 January 2005.

An old blusterer … a big spoilt kid, a pompous windbag … a moron … a gargoyle.
Paddy Sheenan of the *Liverpool Echo* after spending a day with the former *Celebrity Big Brother* contestant at Doncaster, April 2005. In 1990 McCririck had to receive police protection during the Aintree meeting after describing the city as 'a cancer on the face of England'.

I'm a nasty piece of work. I'm not a pleasant chap, I don't have any friends. I bear grudges. I'm malicious. I'm loathed in racing by jockeys, owners and trainers … The public know what a vile, hateful, nasty piece of work I am.
McCririck on himself, quoted in the *Guardian*, 16 June 2005.

… he covets unpopularity like a panto villain whose season never ends … In an unpopularity contest it took Simon Cowell to beat him into second place.
Paul Weaver in the *Guardian*, 16 June 2005.

When a journalist took him to the Ivy he picked his nose and ate its contents. 'An Australian surgeon says it is good for you to pick your nose and eat it,' he explained.
Quoted in the *Guardian*, 16 June 2005.

On the relocation of Royal Ascot to York:

Clare Balding in a big hat is Clare Balding in a big hat.

Giles Smith in *The Times*, 16 June 2005.

On Royal Ascot:

The only event in the sporting calendar in which the word 'diaphanous' is likely to come up in the studio discussions. Even *Match of the Day 2* with Gordon Strachan has never managed a 'diaphanous' and almost certainly never will.

Giles Smith.

Explaining why women do not make good jockeys:

Their bottoms are the wrong shape.

Lester Piggott, quoted in the *Guinness Book of Great Jockeys* (1992).

Brough Scott: What are your immediate thoughts, Walter?

Walter Swinburn: I don't have any immediate thoughts at the moment.

TV commentary.

Describing racing commentators before John McCririck:

A bunch of insular, snobby, sonorous farts twittering on about how lovely the Queen Mother looked at Ascot.

Matthew Norman in the *Evening Standard*, 17 January 2005.

Willie Carson

Top hats look 100 per cent ridiculous on anybody, but on, for example, Willie Carson, it's like attaching a factory chimney to a bungalow.

Giles Smith on the pitfalls of Ascot's royal enclosure dress code; in *The Times*, 16 June 2005.

Ginger McCain

After securing his fourth Aintree triumph (with Amberleigh House):

I'm just an old, broken-down taxi-driver who got lucky in the [Grand] National – again.

Ginger McCain, the trainer of Red Rum; quoted in *The Times*, quotes of the year, 2004.

Julian Wilson

Julian Wilson, McCririck's fagmaster at the rogue's gallery known formally as Harrow ... rendered racing on the Beeb completely unwatchable until the arrival of Clare Balding.

Matthew Norman in the *Evening Standard*, 17 January 2005.

● SAILING

Ellen MacArthur

Ellen is really our very own modern Ancient Mariner, condemned to tell her tale to any wedding guest, internet surfer or Today programme listener she meets.

Marina Hyde, 'MacArthur's tale twice as flat as her dismal, dreary sea', in the *Guardian*, 31 January 2005.

It must be nice for her to talk to someone, but must it be quite so often?

Marina Hyde.

Ellen is a very difficult person to empathize with. She moans and whinges the whole bloody time.

Bob Fisher in the *Guardian*, 8 February 2005.

People have been saying they can't let her win Sports Personality of the Year because she has't got a personality, but ... they let David Beckham win it, didn't they?

Jan Raven (impersonator of MacArthur on *Dead Ringers*) in the *Guardian*, 8 February 2005.

I don't think she has 'friends' as such, although she does have admirers – most of them French.
Bob Fisher.

MacArthur has kept a weblog detailing her emotional highs and lows. This may have been a mistake. Take her collision with a whale, an event with great literary potential: 'I saw a whale very, very close to the boat ... I didn't see its tail but it must have been about 30 feet long' ... Herman Melville got 300,000 words out of something similar.
Stephen Moss in the *Guardian*, 8 February 2005.

● SNOOKER

We will be with you a little early on Monday because apparently it is an iron rule of public service broadcasting on a bank holiday that nothing is allowed to disturb the snooker.
Jeremy Paxman, BBC2 *Newsnight*, 30 April 2005.

Steve Davis

I'm a rancid old man!
Steve Davis, aged 47, after being beaten 9–2 by Stephen Maguire, 23, in the UK snooker championship.

Alex Higgins

Reported comment by Higgins to Stephen Hendry before a match:
Hello: I'm the devil.
Quoted by John Rawling in the *Guardian*, 2 May 2005.

Shaun Murphy

Alongside fellow snooker professional Stephen Lee and England test batsman Robert Key, Shaun takes his place on the Army Council of the Provisional Butcher's Boy wing of British sport.
Matthew Norman in the *Evening Standard*, 9 May 2005 (*see also* page 183).

... at the current rate of progress Shaun will make Nicholas Soames look like Nicolas Anelka by next spring.

Matthew Norman goes on: 'The Rotherham-based player is also a born-again Christian who will remain a virgin until his marriage to Clare in July when one hopes (for her sake) that the Murphy family winch will be brought out of storage.'

Ronnie O'Sullivan

On O'Sullivan's style of smoking a cigarette:

... like someone in a Glasgow bus queue circa 1955.

Martin Kelner in the *Guardian*, 2 May 2005. 'Sucking ... on a tab end, gripped between thumb and index finger.'

Matthew Stevens

Is it me or does he look like he's auditioning for the role of The Only Gay in The Village? All he needs is a rubber waistcoat and he'd be there.

Derek 'Robbo' Robson, The Tees Mouth, on bbc.co.uk, April 2005. 'Robbo' described Steven Lee's and Matthew Stevens's hairstyles at the 2005 Embassy World Snooker Championships as 'two of the poorest choices of barnet in the history of indoor sport'.

[Stevens's] natural expression is that of a man who may have mislaid his winning lottery ticket.

Paul Weaver in the *Guardian*, 3 May 2005, describing Stevens's loss to Shaun Murphy in the final of the 2005 Embassy World Snooker Championships, the first qualifier ever to win the world title.

Willie Thorne

I don't know if there is something wrong with my TV – I had a new set-top box installed recently – but his [Willie Thorne's] head seems to be growing. Maybe that is what they mean by Sky Plus … In its present condition, the Thorne napper is reminiscent of the Mekon in the Eagle … or, in view of Willie's deep mahogany hue, the Mekon newly returned from a fortnight playing golf in the Algarve.

Martin Kelner in the *Guardian*, 2 May 2005.

Jimmy White

His marriage ... has suffered grievously from his habit ... of nipping out for a pack of fags, and returning a week later with no memory of anything beyond the first 27 pints.

Matthew Norman in the *Evening Standard*, 14 February 2005.

Extra security guards have been drafted into the Masters snooker tournament to prevent a repeat of last year's disturbances when White fans put off his opponents by deliberately breaking wind between shots. 'The farters will not be tolerated,' the Whirlwind himself has warned.

'Backpages' in the *Guardian*, 21 February 2005.

On spotting the 'Whirlwind' in a Dublin street:

One hundred and eighty!

Footballer Jason McAteer yells the wrong catchphrase; quoted in the *Daily Mail*, 9 March 2005.

PICTURE CREDITS

Every effort has been made to trace the sources of these pictures. Should there be any unintentional omissions the publisher will be happy to include them in a future edition.

2 Empics; 6 Empics; 15 Getty Images; 22 Empics; 25 Empics; 29 Getty Images; 33 Empics; 34 Action Images; 40 Empics; 50 Empics; 56 Empics; 65 Action Images; 74 Empics; 84 Empics; 100–1 Empics; 103 Action Images; 110 Empics; 112 Empics; 123 Empics; 134 Empics; 136–7 Empics; 153 Empics; 157 Empics; 159 Empics; 170 Empics; 172 Getty Images; 175 Action Images; 178–9 Empics; 183 Empics; 191 Getty Images; 192–3 Empics; 208 Empics; 221 Getty Images; 227 SWpix; 230 Empics; 239 Action Images; 244 Getty Images; 249 Action Images; 251 Empics; 256 Empics; 277 Getty Images; 280–1 Empics; 285 Empics; 294 Empics; 296 Empics; 307 Empics; 314 Getty Images; 327 Reuters; 341 Empics.

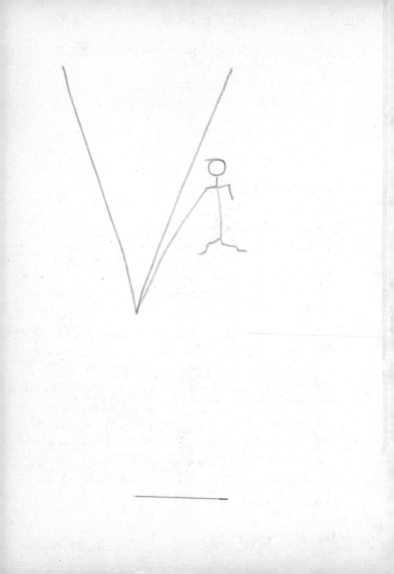

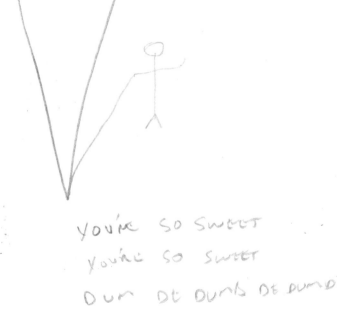

YOU'RE SO SWEET
YOU'RE SO SWEET
DUM DE DUMB DE DUMB
DE DITES

X